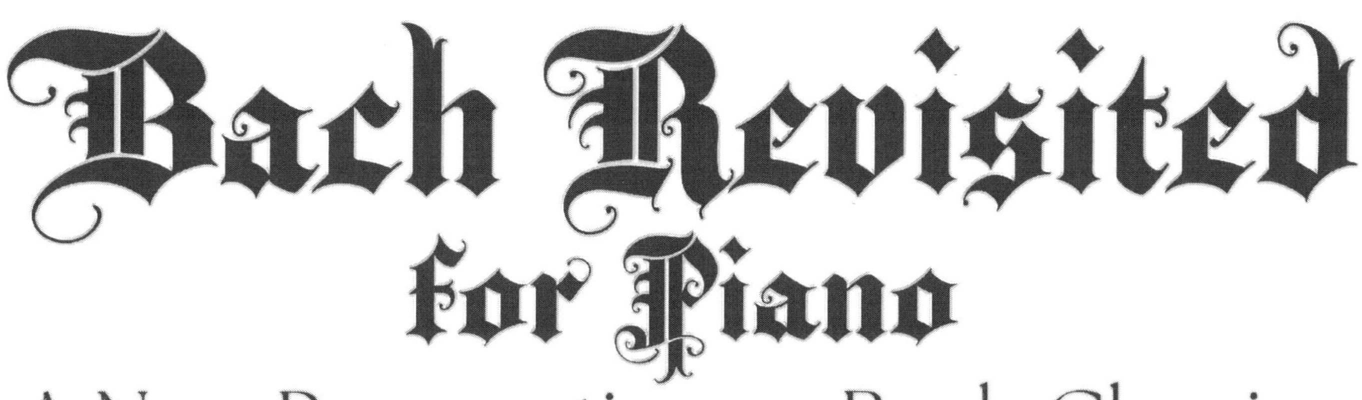

A New Perspective on Bach Classics

Bryce Russell

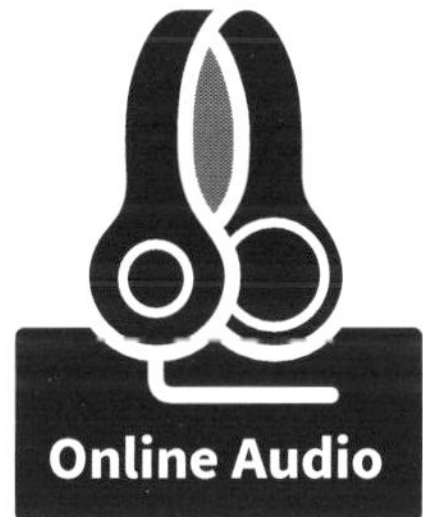

To access the online audio, scan the QR code above or go to:
WWW.MELBAY.COM/31199MEB

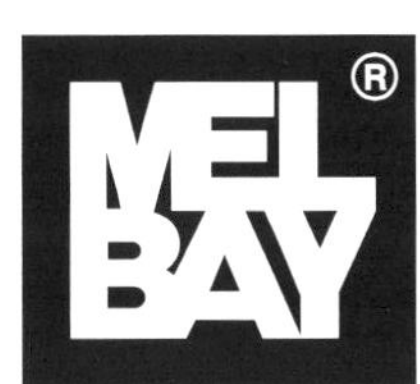

WWW.MELBAY.COM

Preface

What if Bach wrote music during a different era? That is the subject of this collection. Twelve of Johann Sebastian Bach's (J. S. Bach) most famous and melodious pieces arranged in the style of Ravel among others, adapting the characteristics of impressionism with Bach's aesthetic. Blending these two styles provides a brand-new twist on Bach's music, and will be a unique perspective welcomed by musicians, students, teachers, and audiences everywhere.

Included are popular favorites from the French and English suites, *Well-Tempered Clavier*, *Cantata BWV 147*, and from the *Notebooks for Anna Magdalena Bach*, a range of pieces for all skill levels. Likewise, they have been left in their original keys to make them familiar to players and listeners, but with the fusion of styles like previously mentioned.

Different interpretations of performance exist around Bach's music, so a range of suggested metronome indications have been given, which should give an approximate range of tempos to obtain a closer rendition of each piece. Likewise, the pedal indications can be adapted as well with different make/models of piano but should be used with discretion to keep the elegant and dream-like quality retained that these arrangements intend.

Enjoy this new perspective on Bach's great and powerful music and experience a different dimension of these timeless classics. I would like to thank all my friends and family for the support over the years, and another thanks goes to the fantastic staff at Mel Bay Publications. Without everyone's wonderful support this project would not be possible.

Bryce Russell

Bryce Russell

Contents

Bourrée

from Overture in F Major
BWV 820

Johann Sebastian Bach
Arranged by Bryce Russell

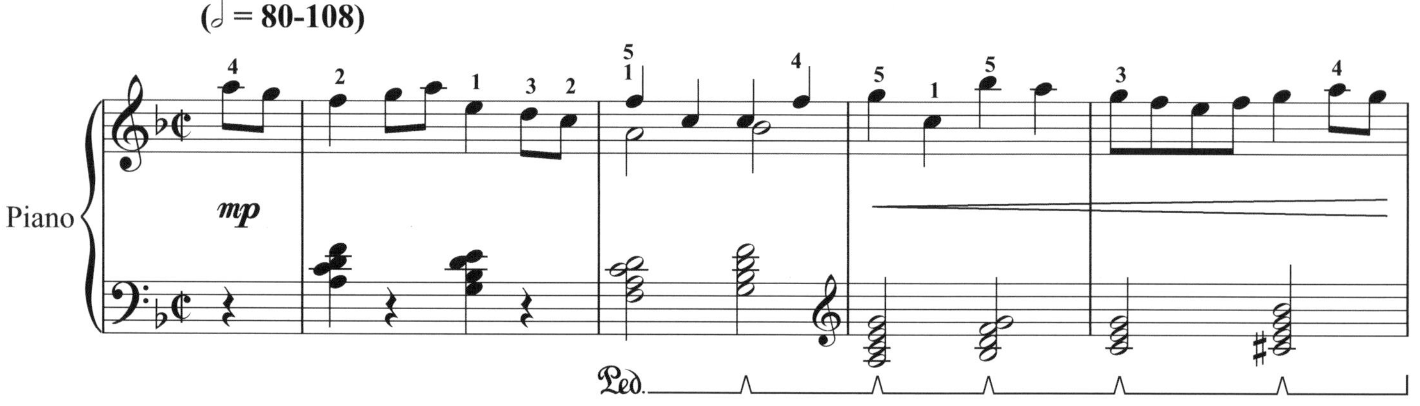

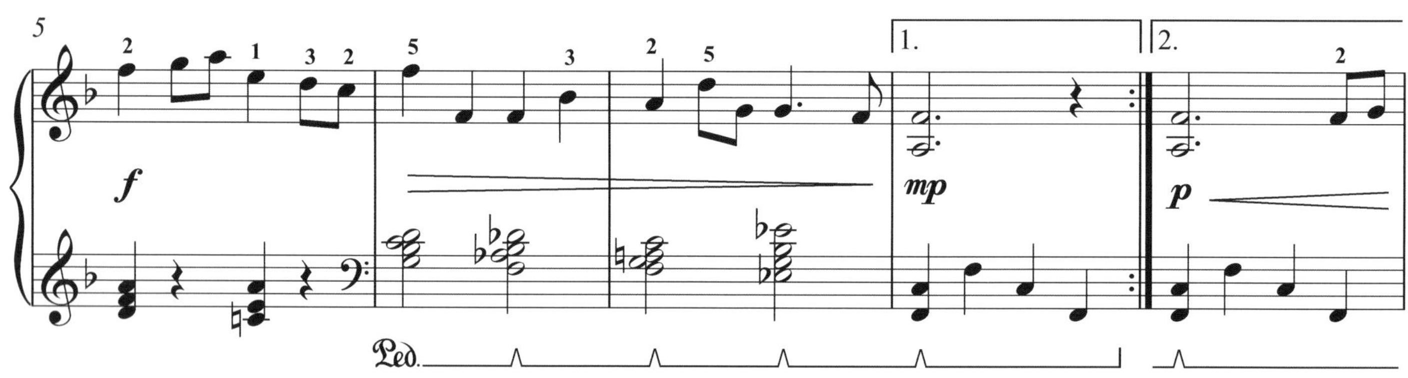

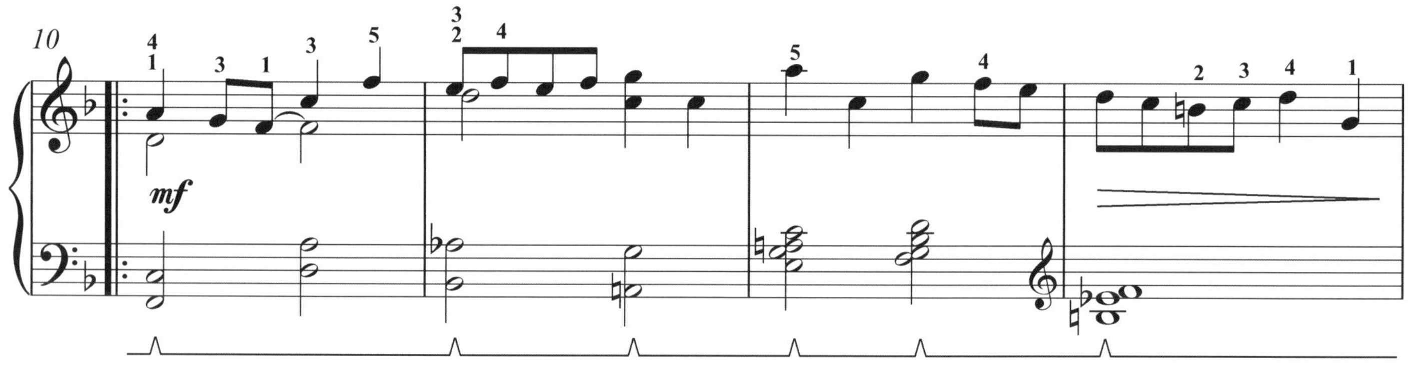

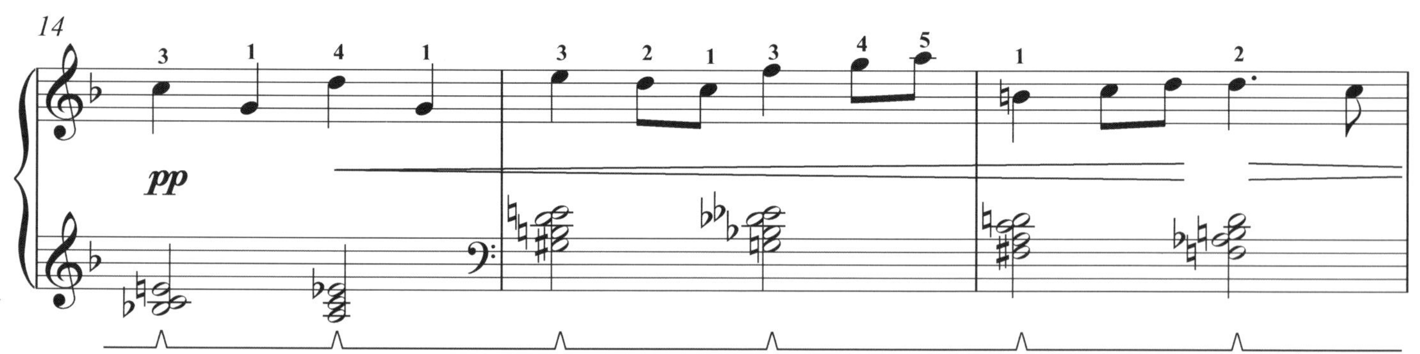

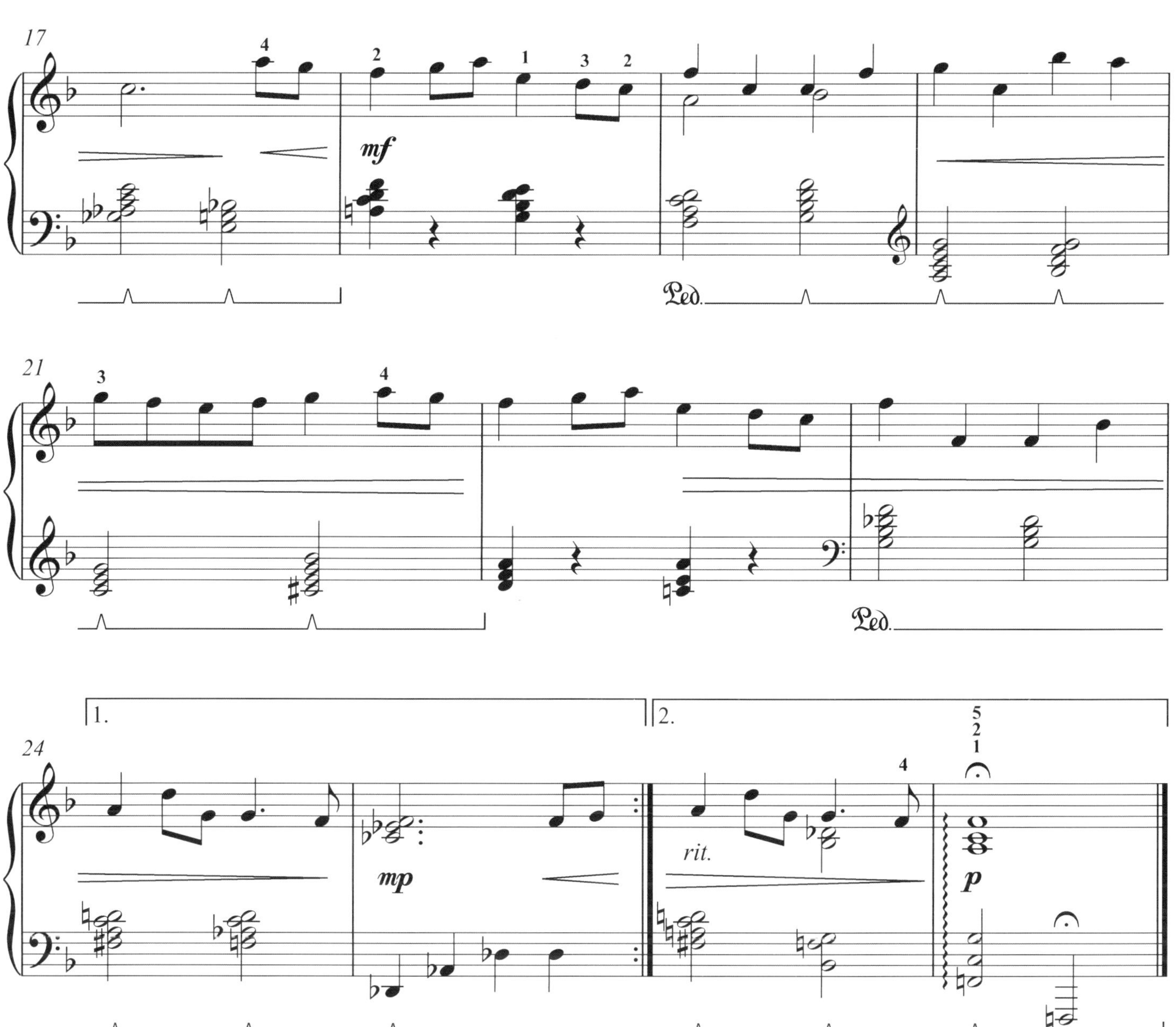

mf
Ped.
Ped.
1.
2.
mp
rit.
p

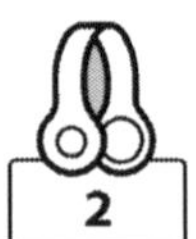

Courante

from Suite in E♭ Major
BWV 819

Johann Sebastian Bach
Arranged by Bryce Russell

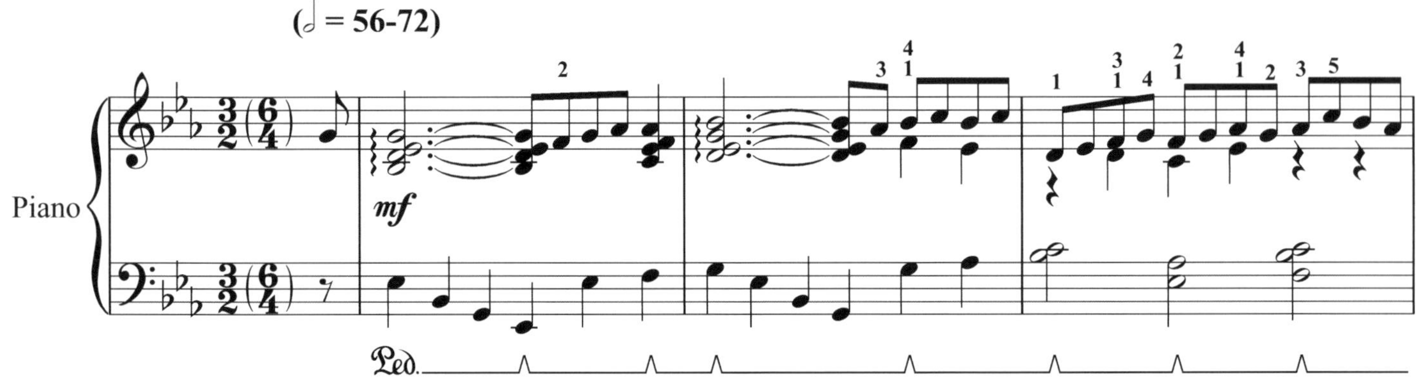

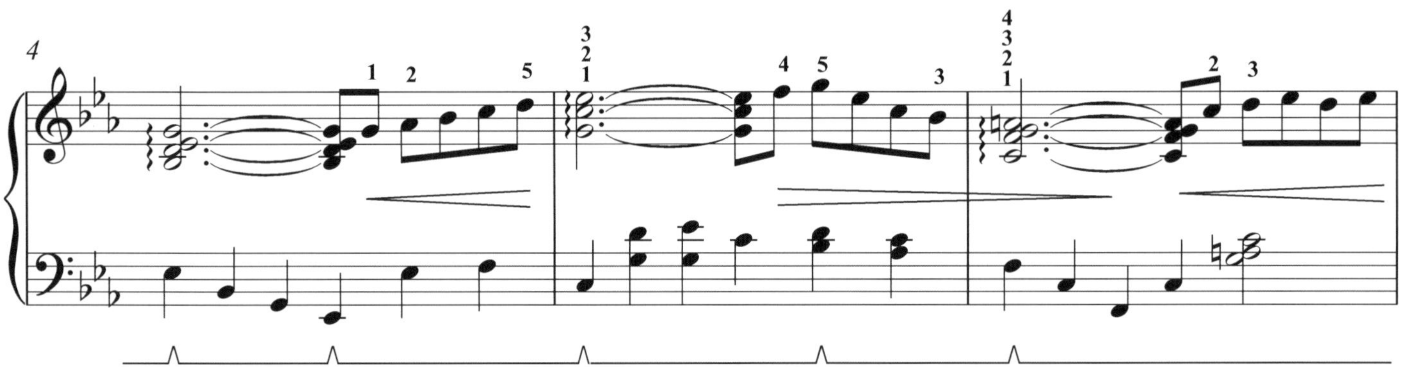

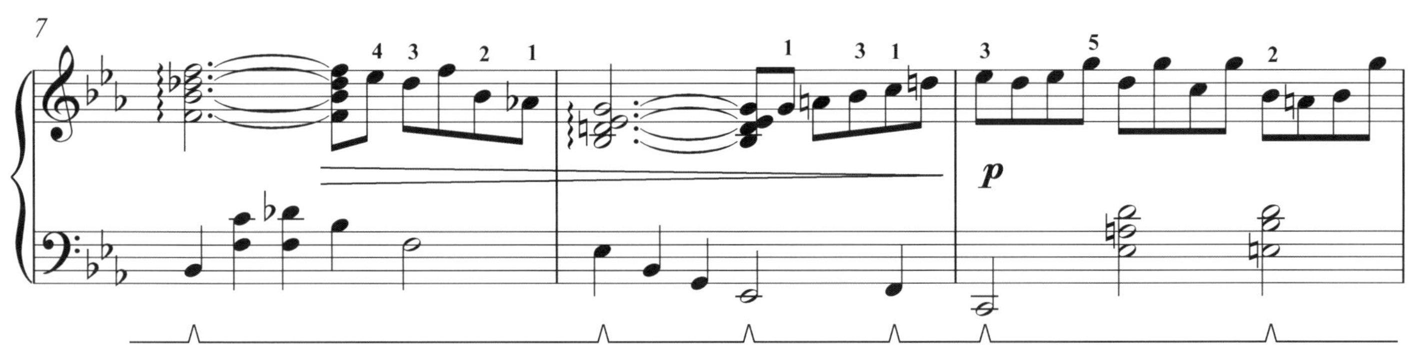

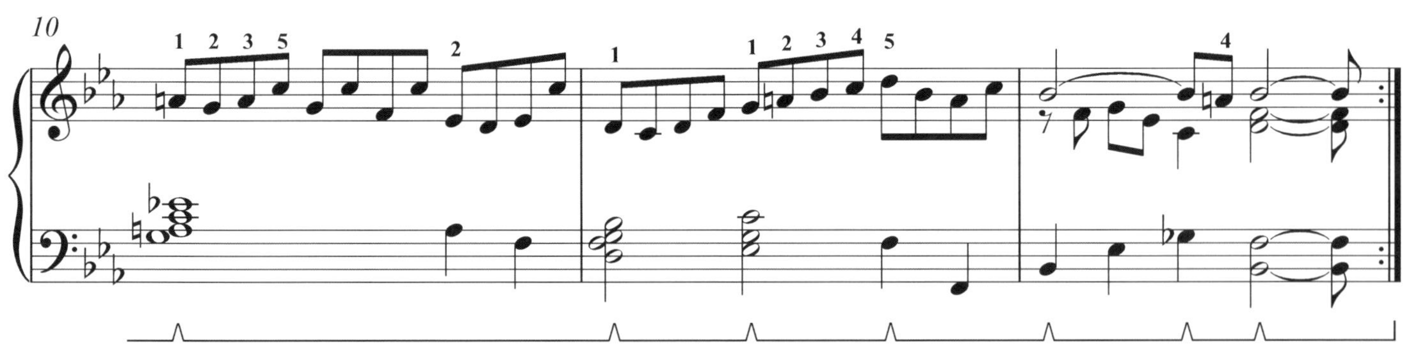

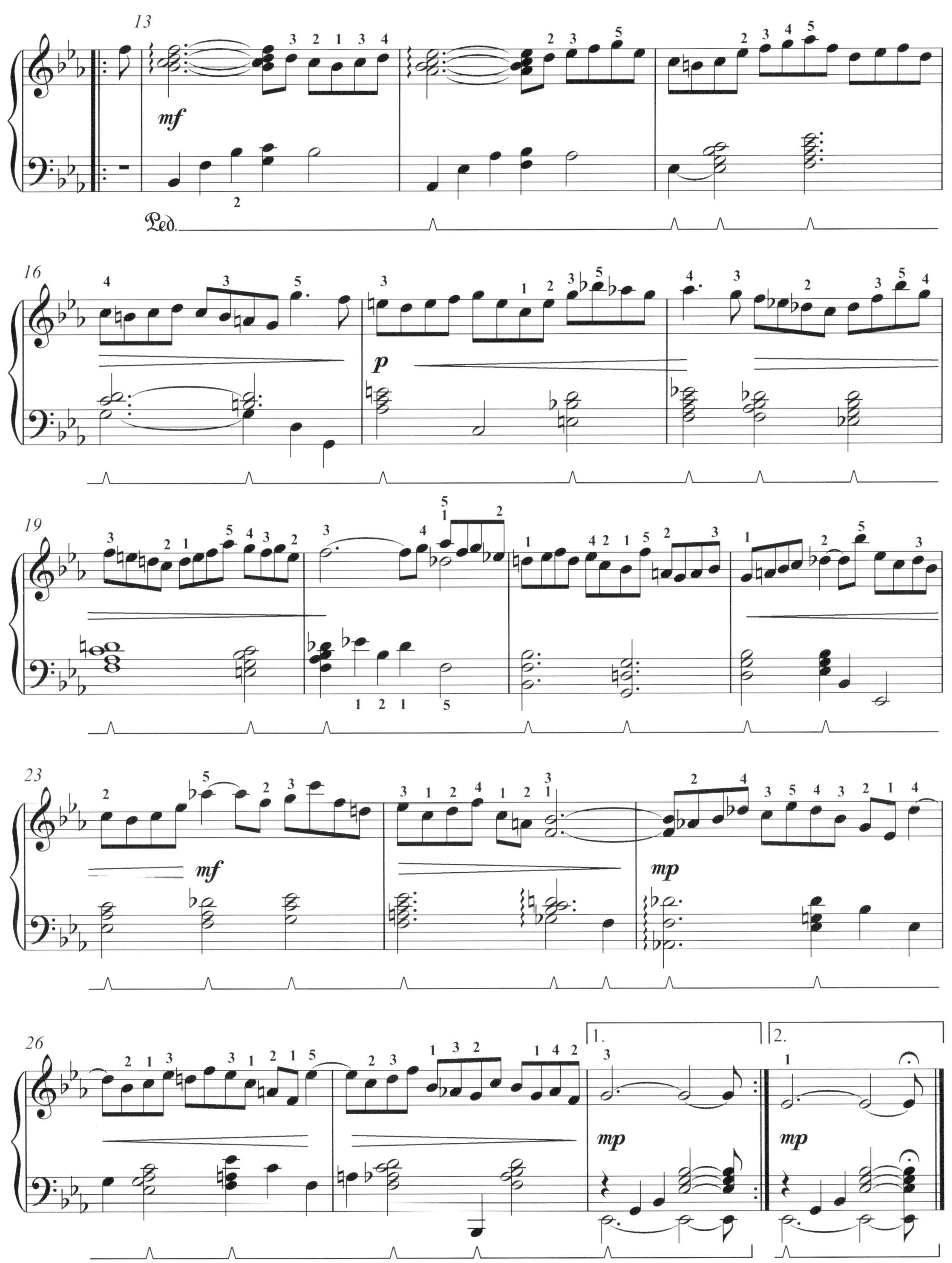

13
mf
Ped.
16
p
19
23
mf
mp
26
1.
2.
mp
mp

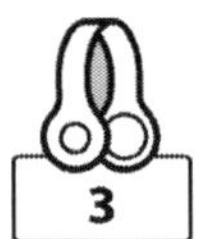

Gavotte

from French Suite No. 5
BWV 816

Johann Sebastian Bach
Arranged by Bryce Russell

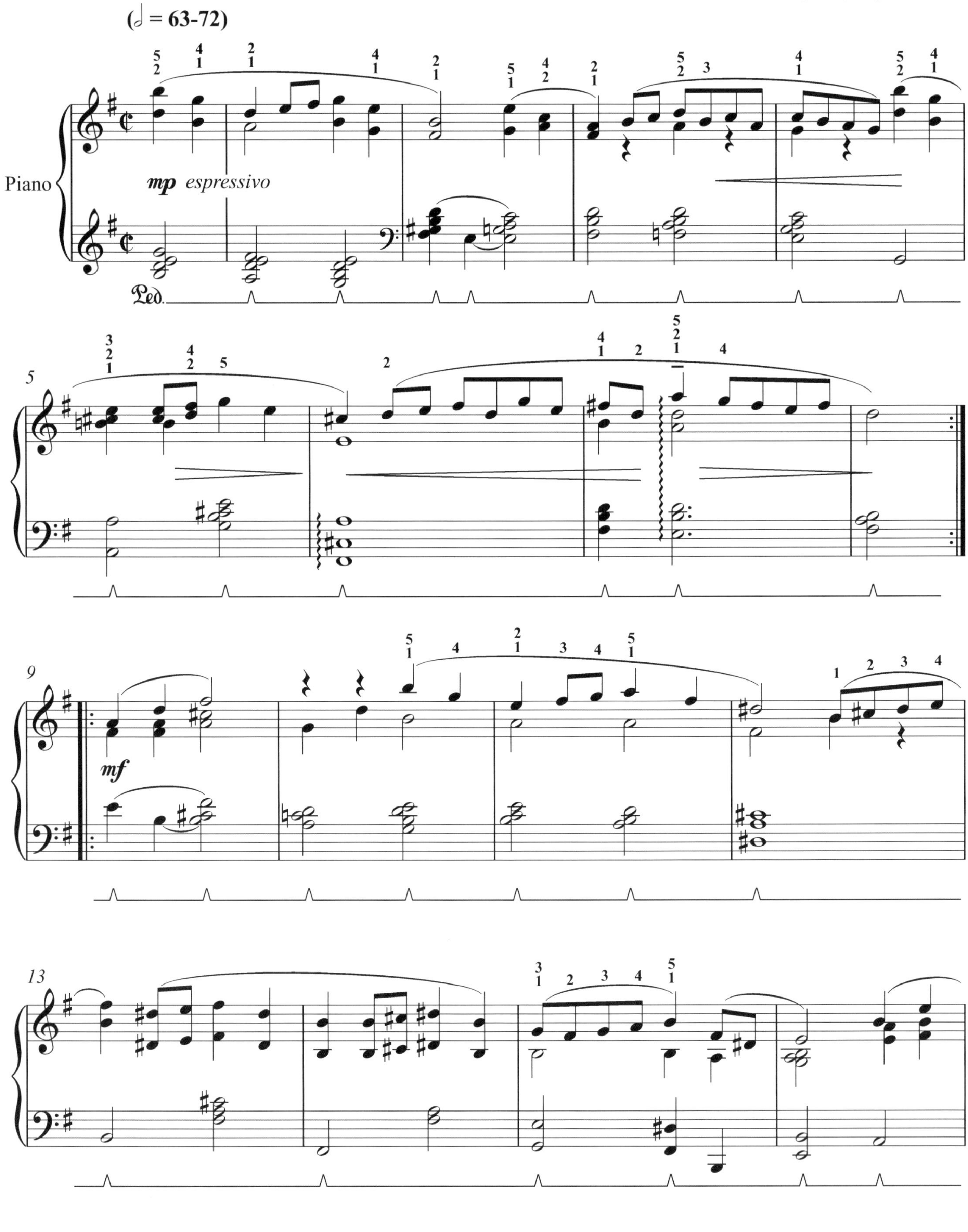

(𝅗𝅥 = 63-72)

Piano

mp espressivo

Ped.

5

9

mf

13

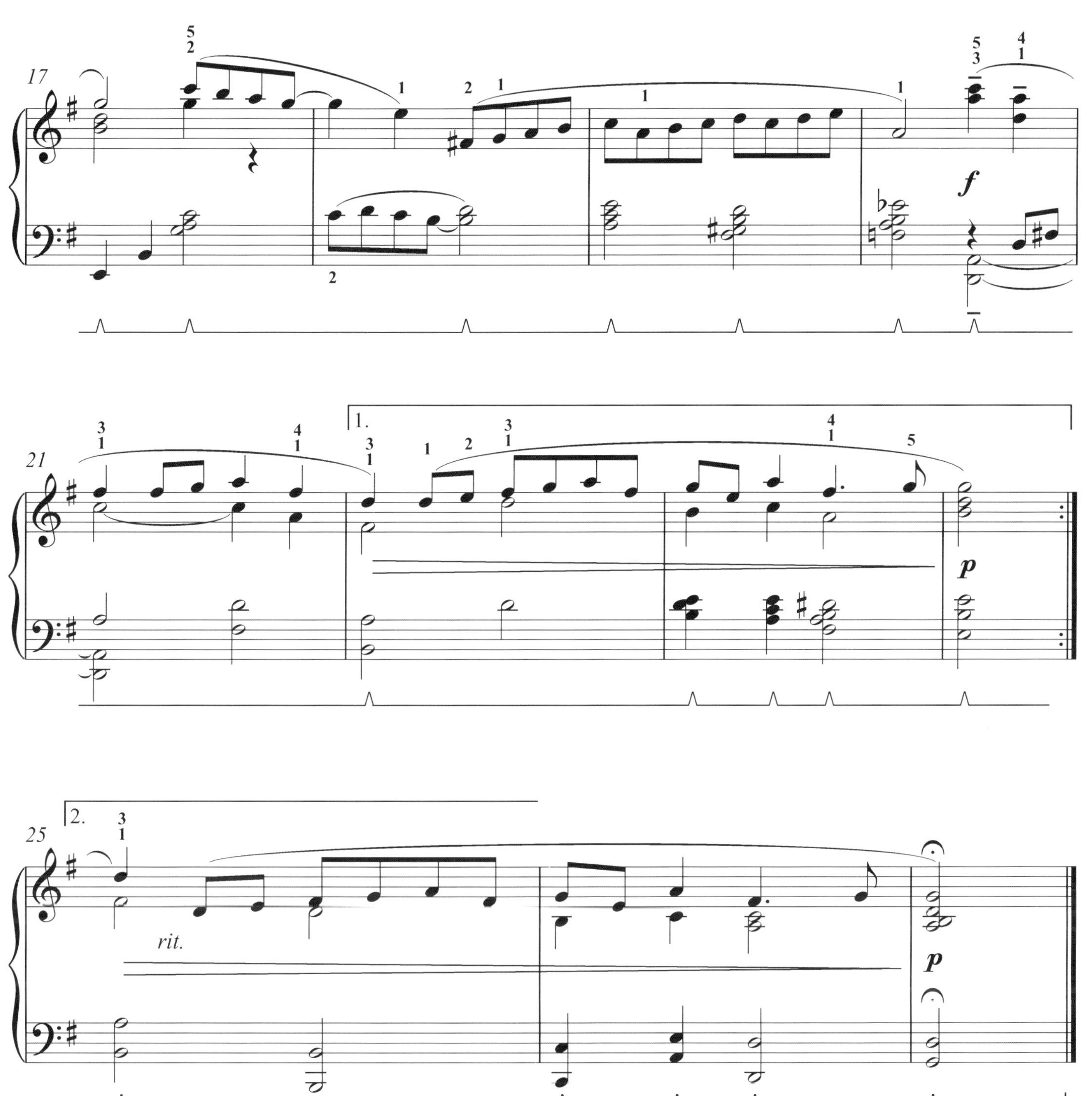
17
21
1.
25
2.
rit.

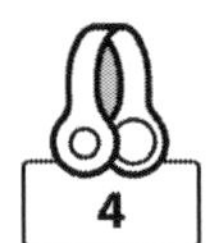

Gigue

from French Suite No. 2
BWV 813

Johann Sebastian Bach
Arranged by Bryce Russell

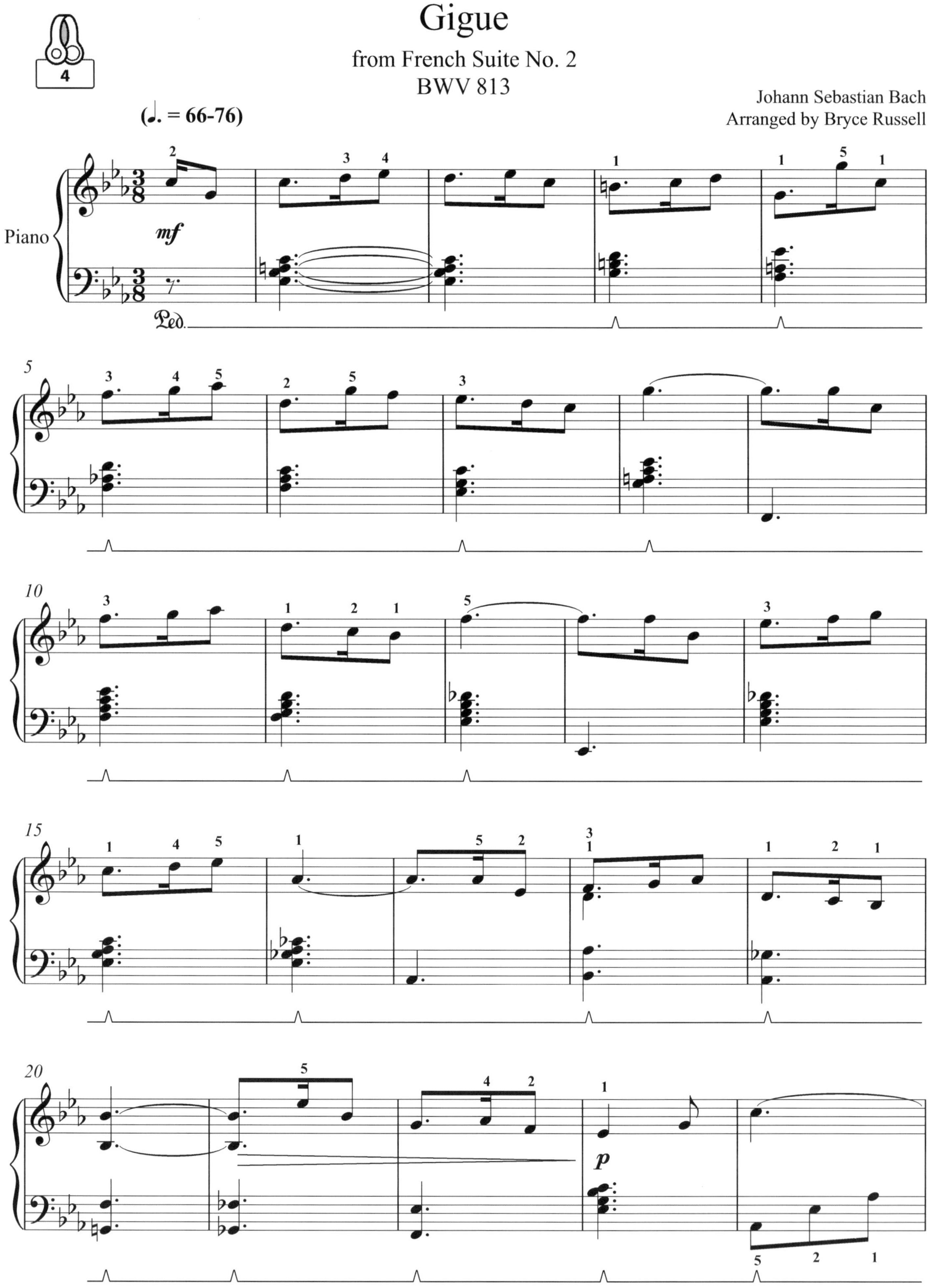

(♩. = 66-76)

Piano

mf

Ped.

p

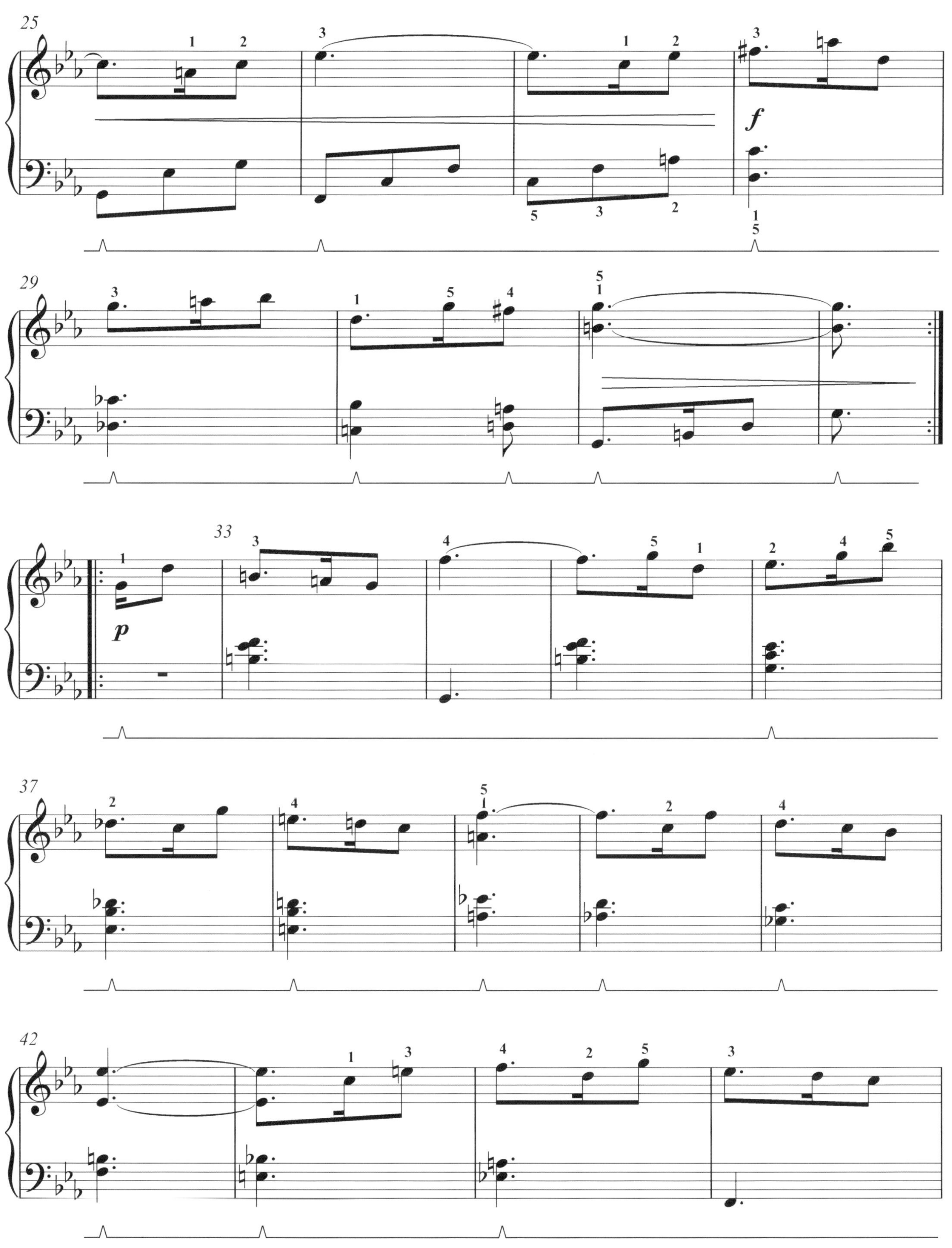

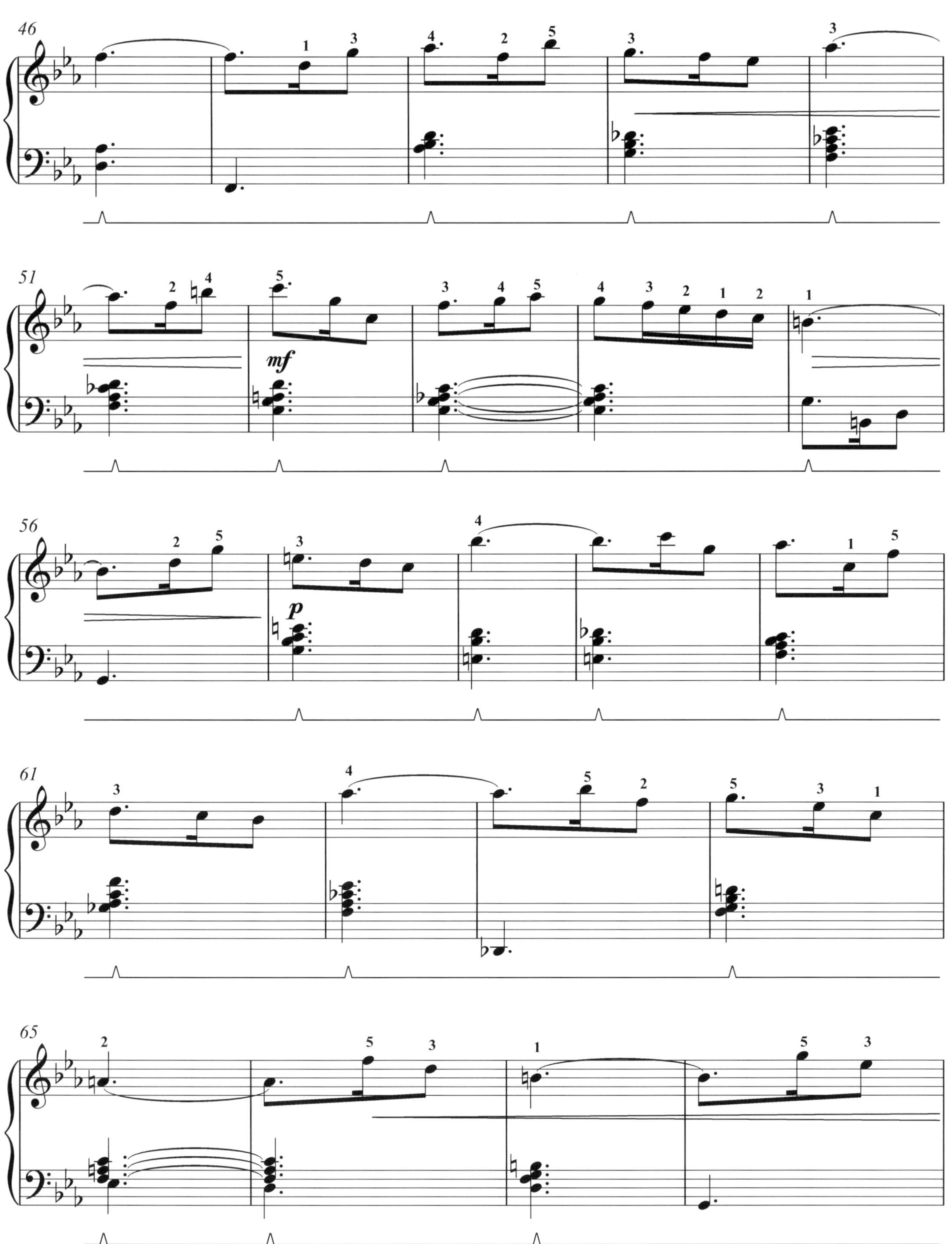
46
51
mf
56
p
61
65

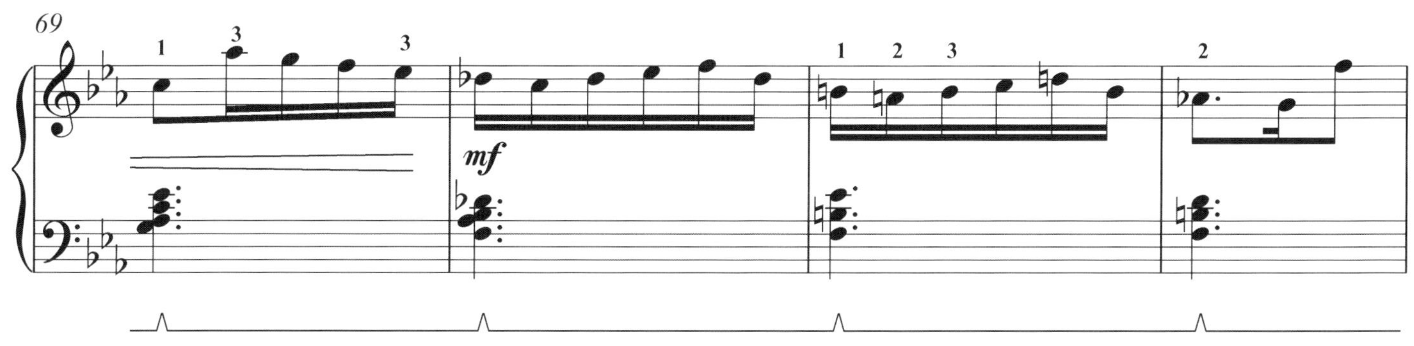
69
1
3
3
mf
1
2
3
2
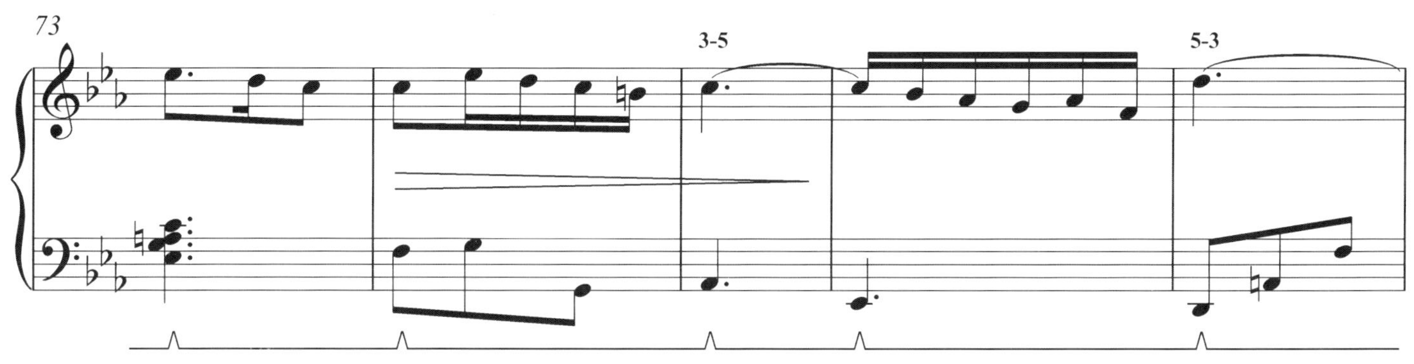
73
3-5
5-3
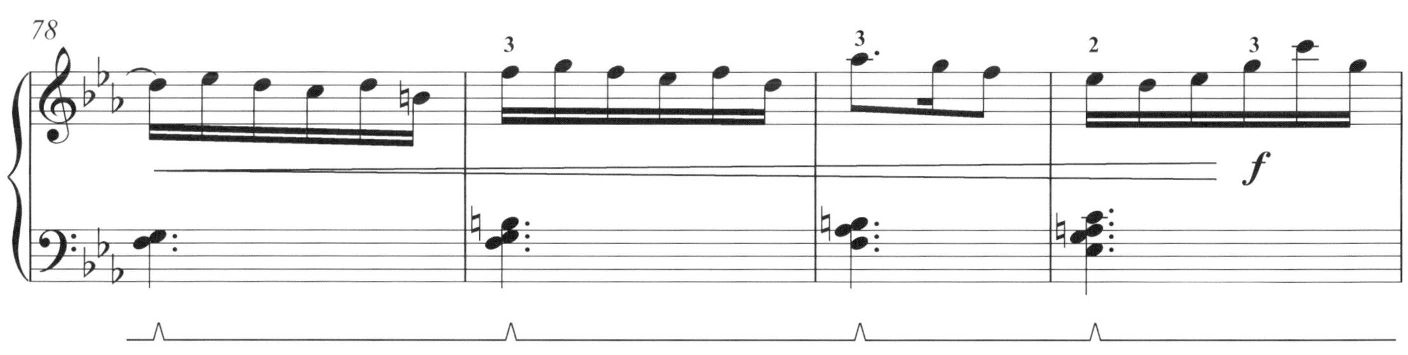
78
3
3
2
3
f
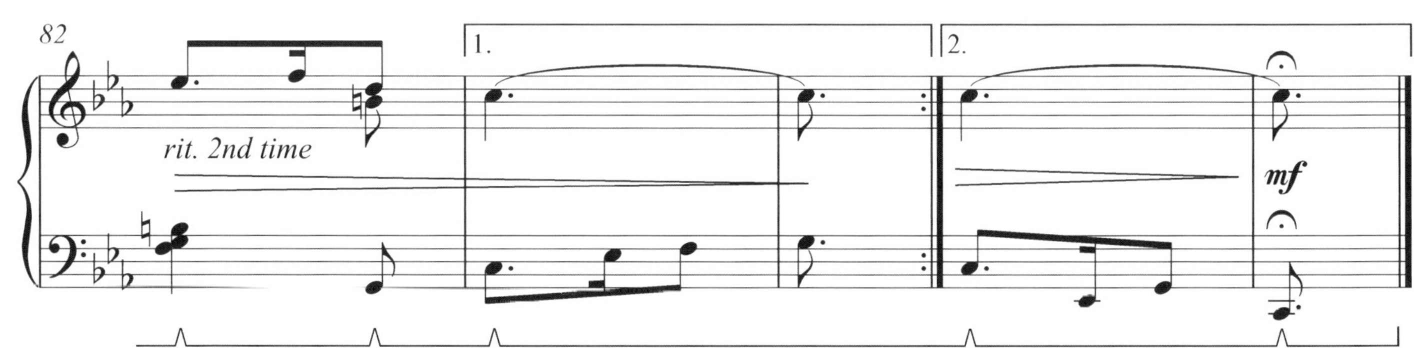
82
1.
2.
rit. 2nd time
mf

"Jesu, Joy of Man's Desiring"

Chorale from Cantata BWV 147

Johann Sebastian Bach
Arranged by Bryce Russell

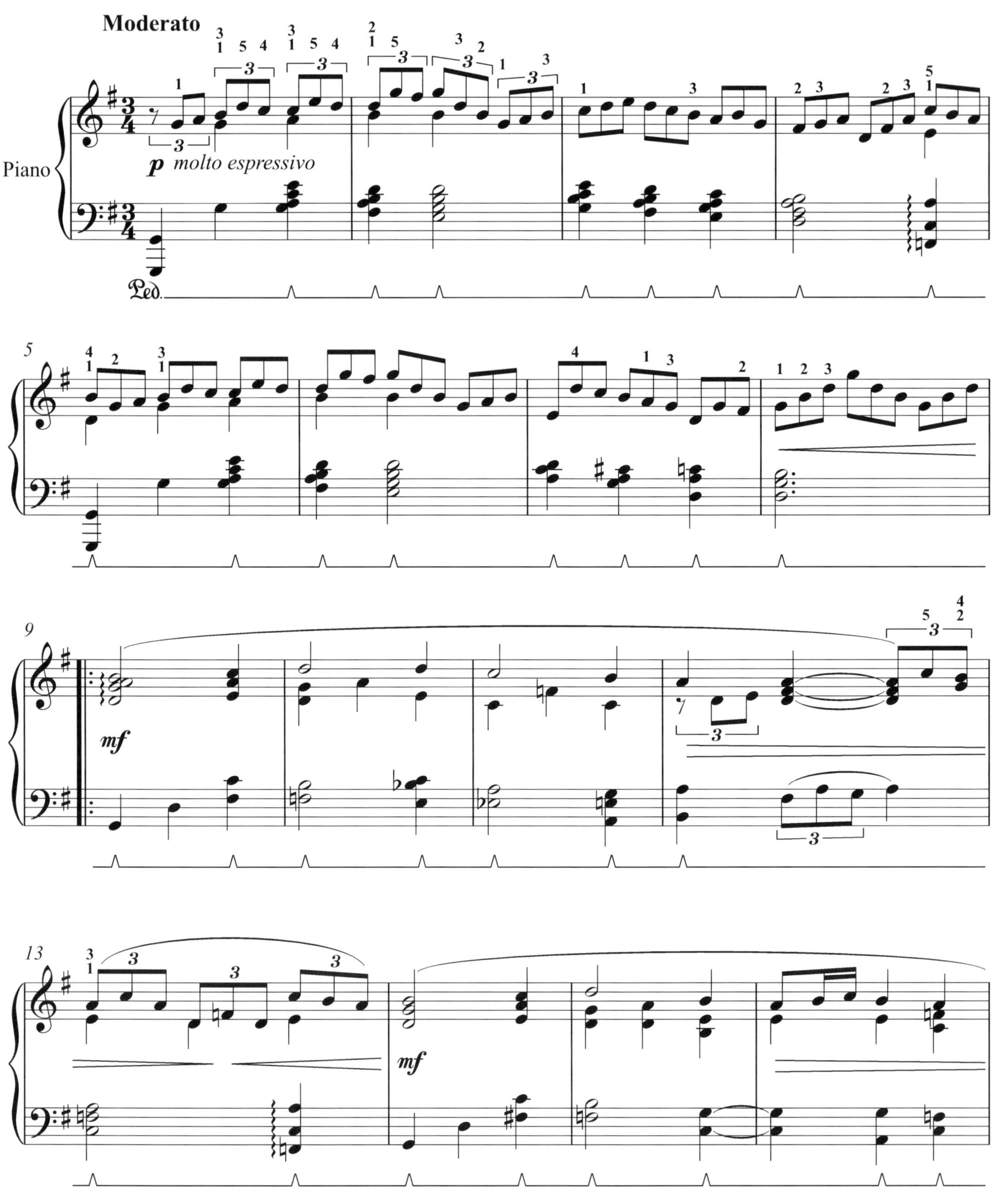

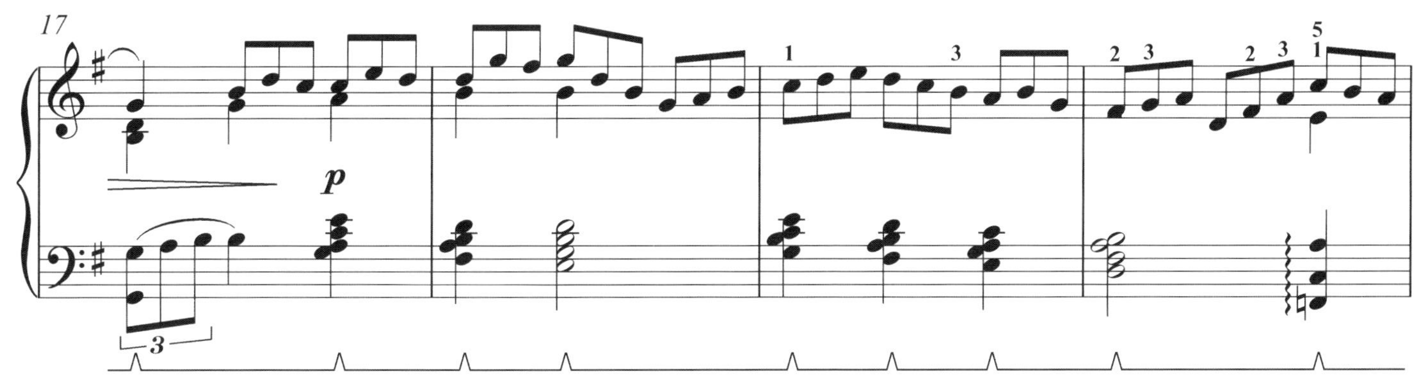
17
p

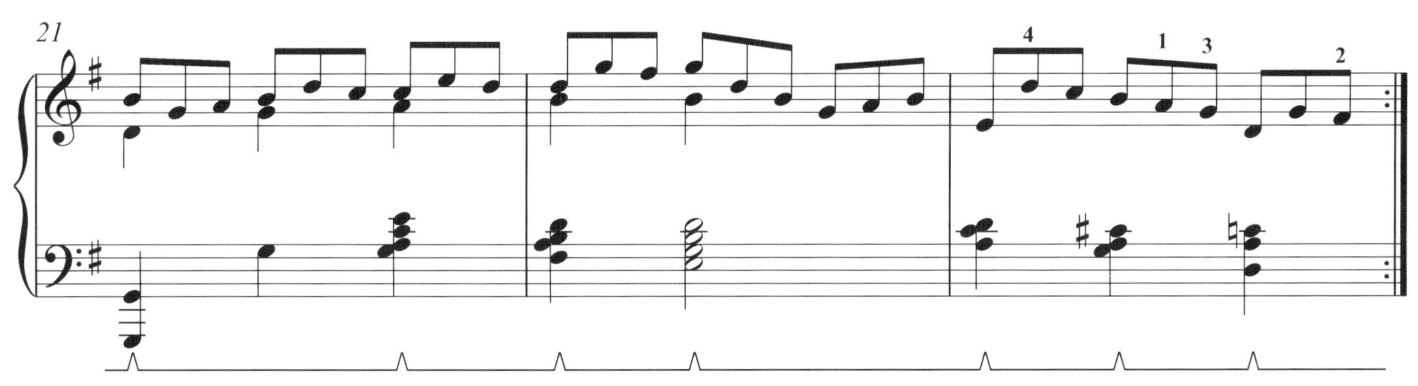
21

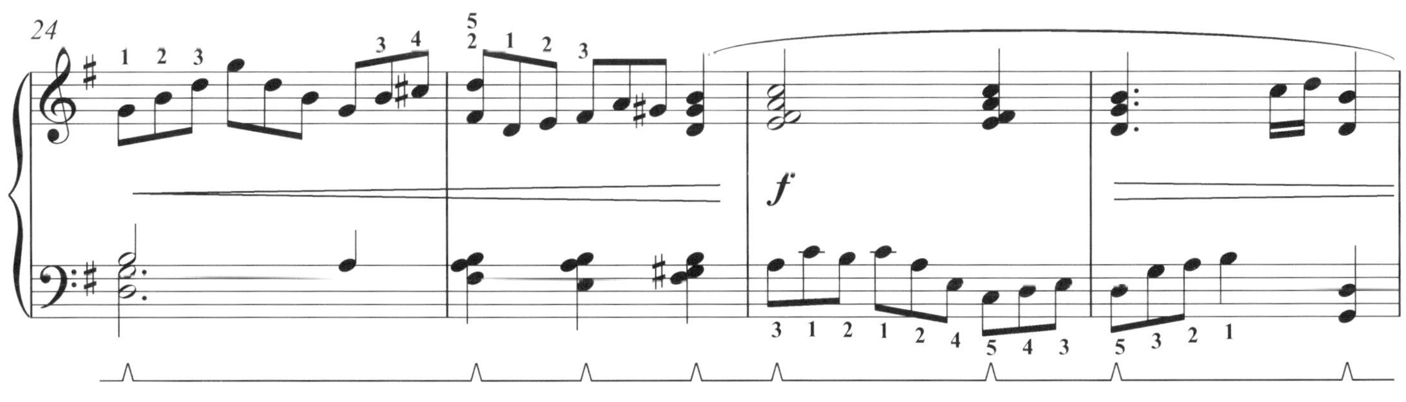
24
f

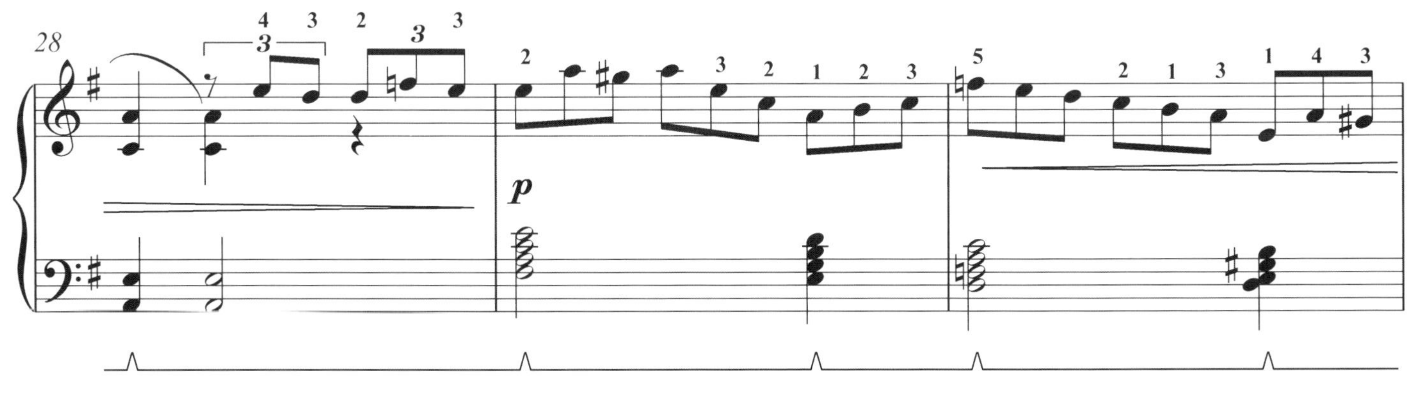
28
p

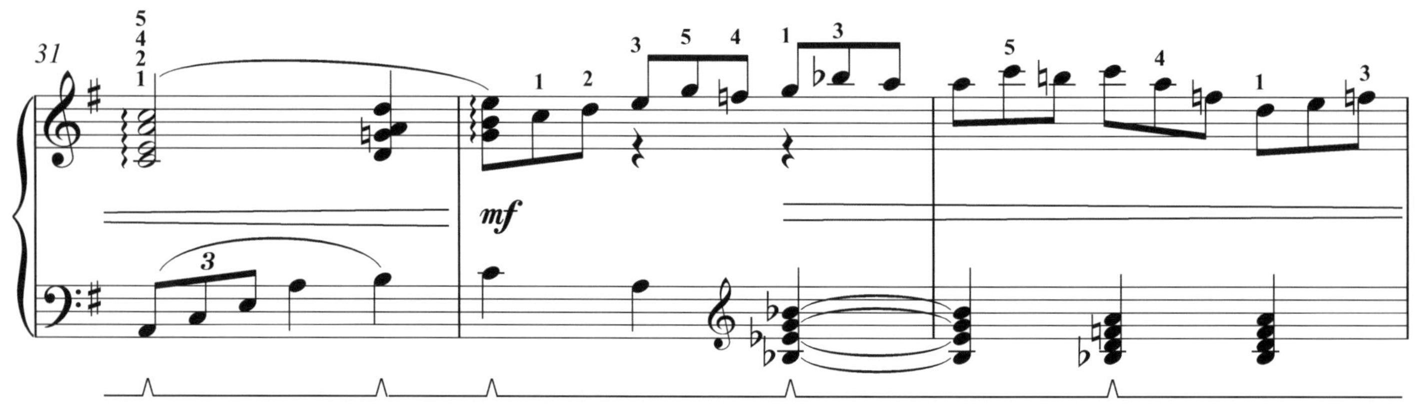
31
mf
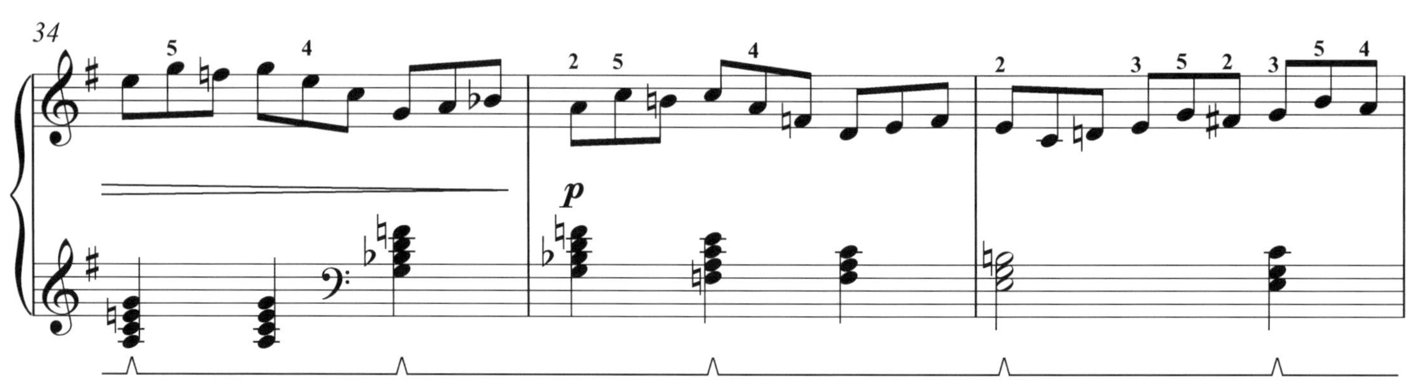
34
p
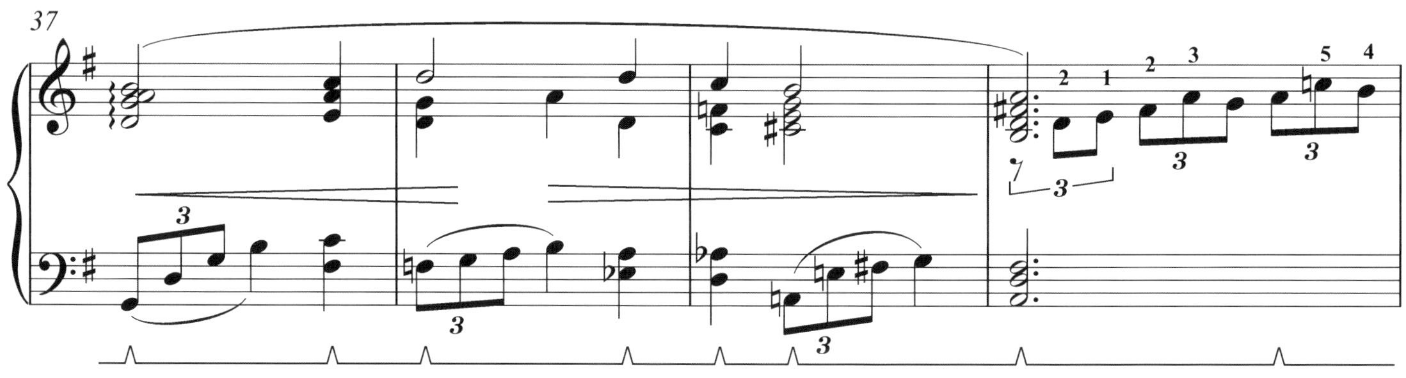
37
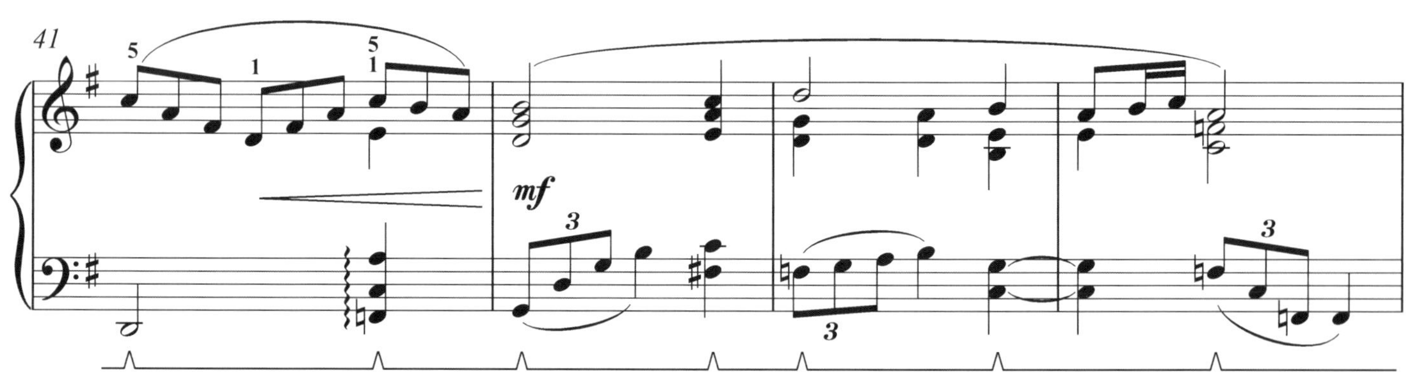
41
mf

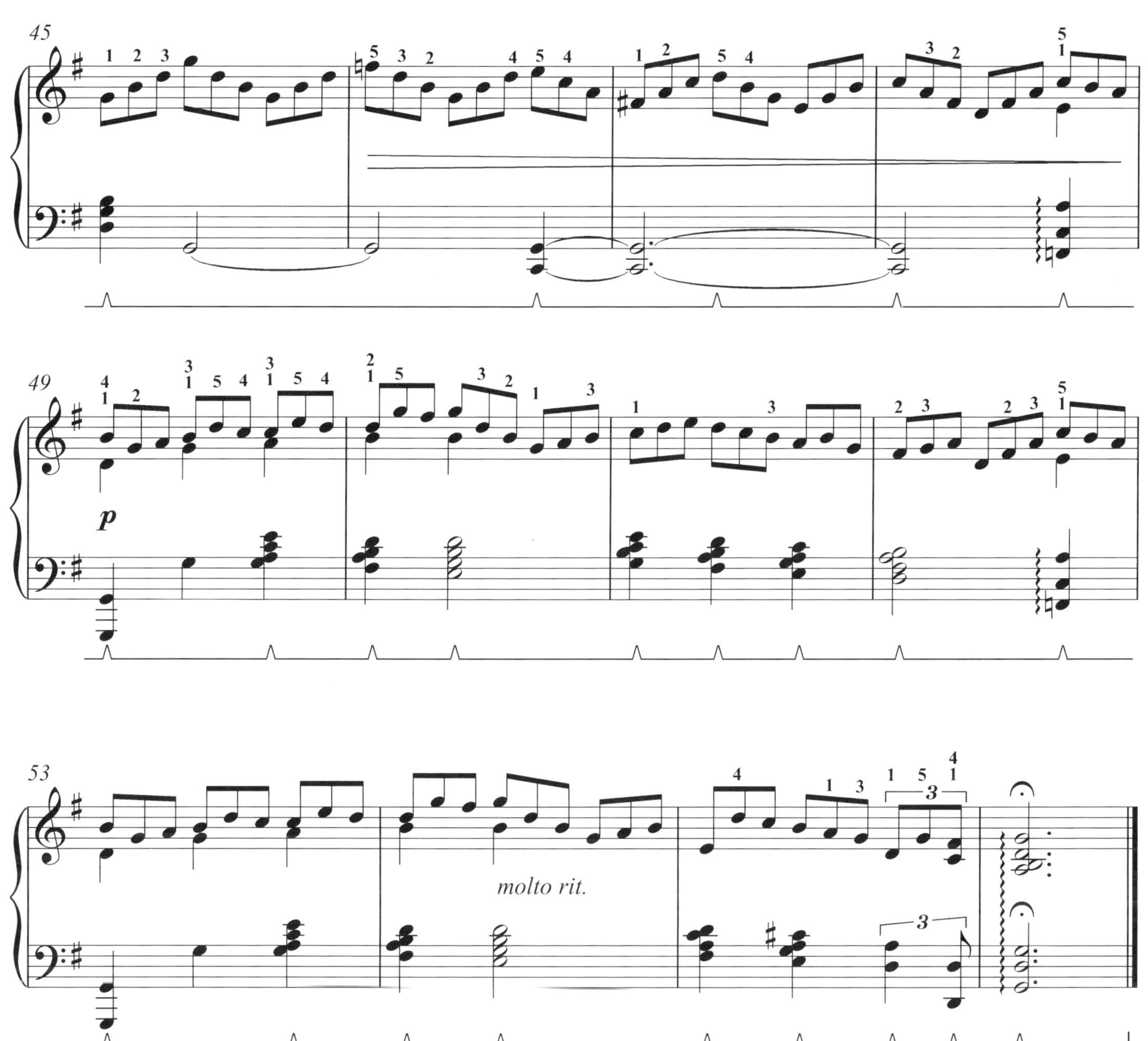
45
49
p
53
molto rit.

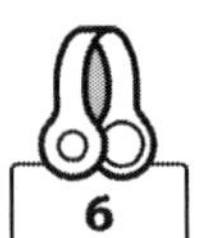

Menuet

from the Notebook for Anna Magdalena Bach 1725
BWV Anh. 113

Johann Sebastian Bach
Arranged by Bryce Russell

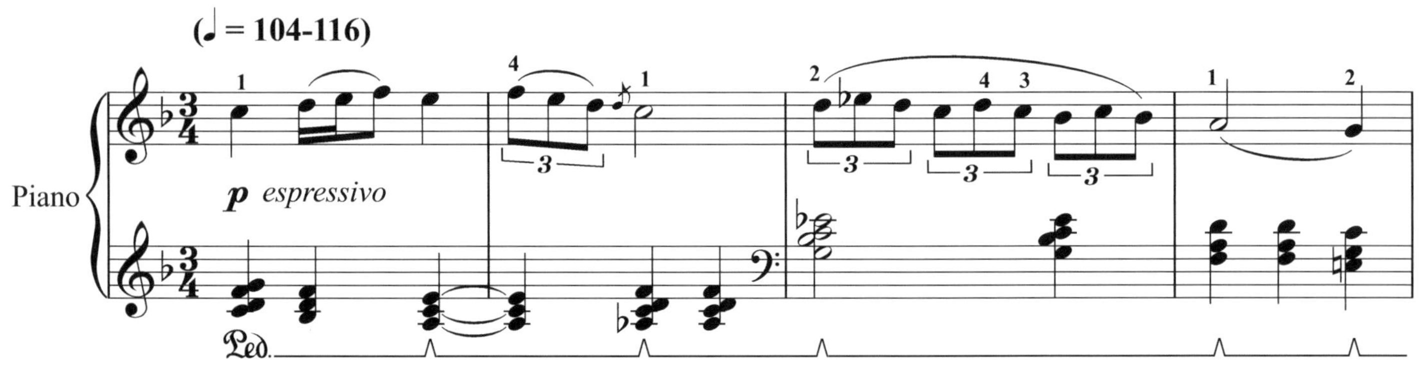

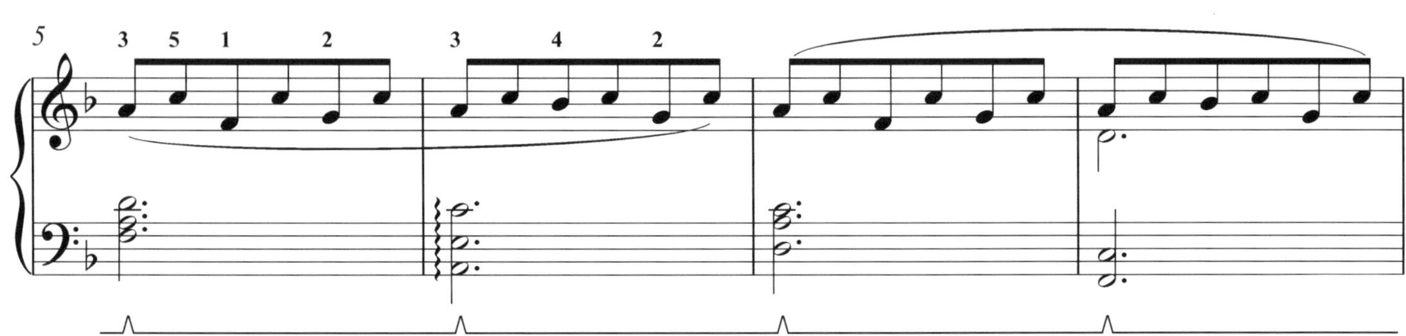

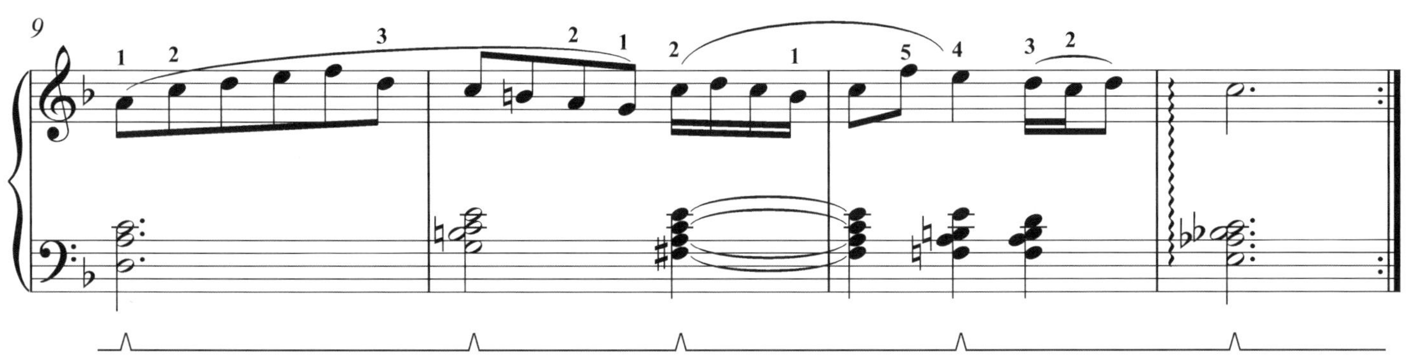

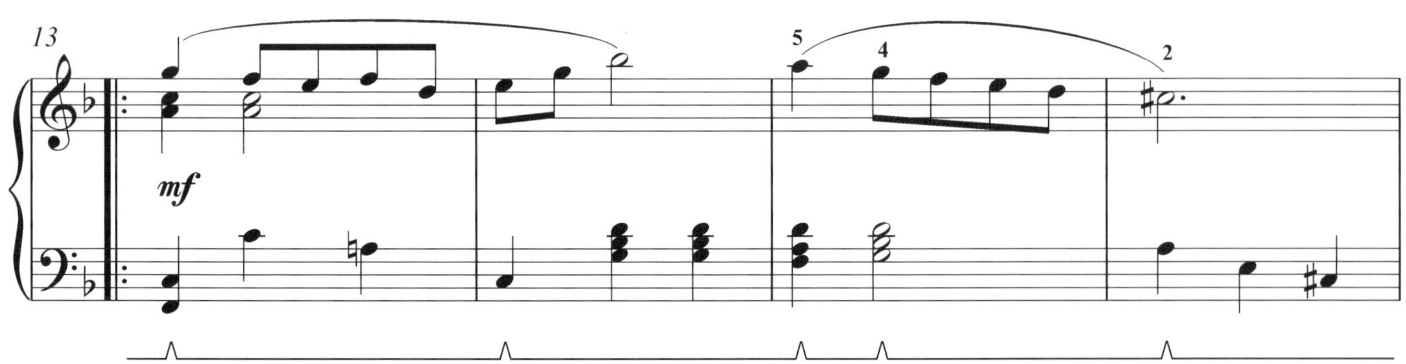

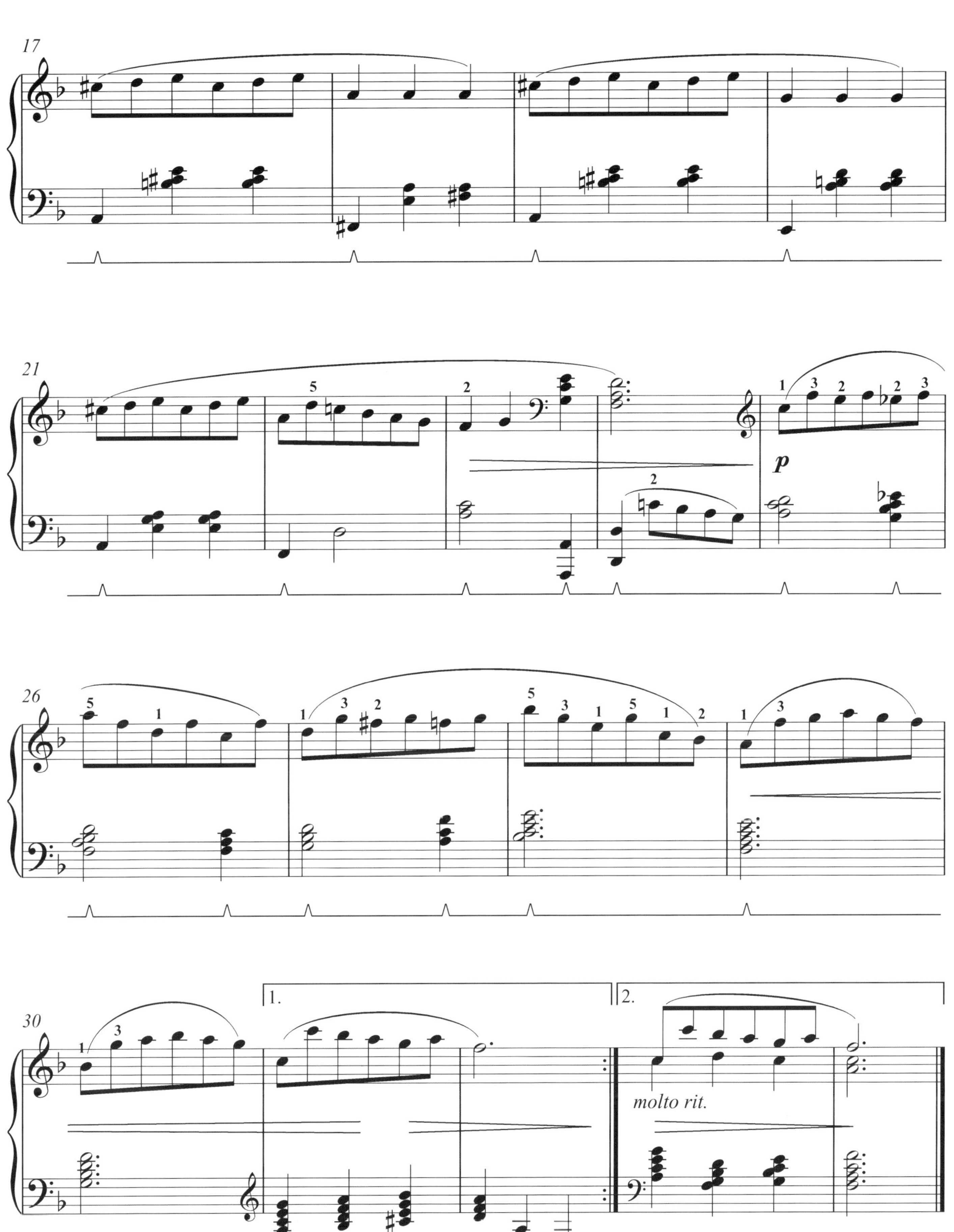

17
21
p
26
30
1.
2.
molto rit.

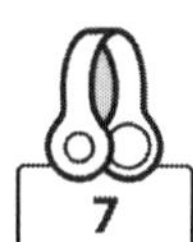

Menuet

from the Notebook for Anna Magdalena Bach 1725

BWV Anh. 116

Johann Sebastian Bach

Arranged by Bryce Russell

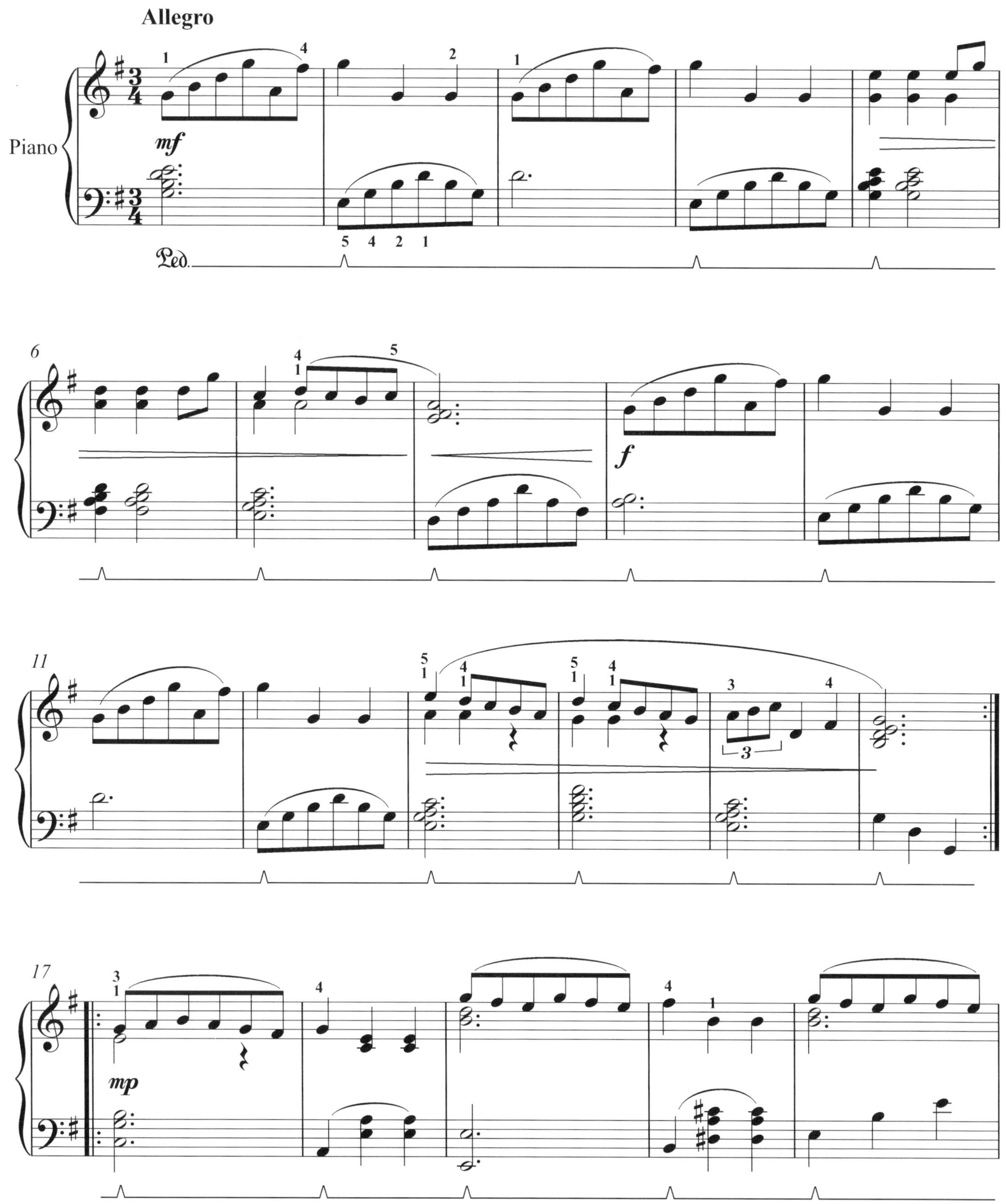

Allegro

Piano

mf

f

mp

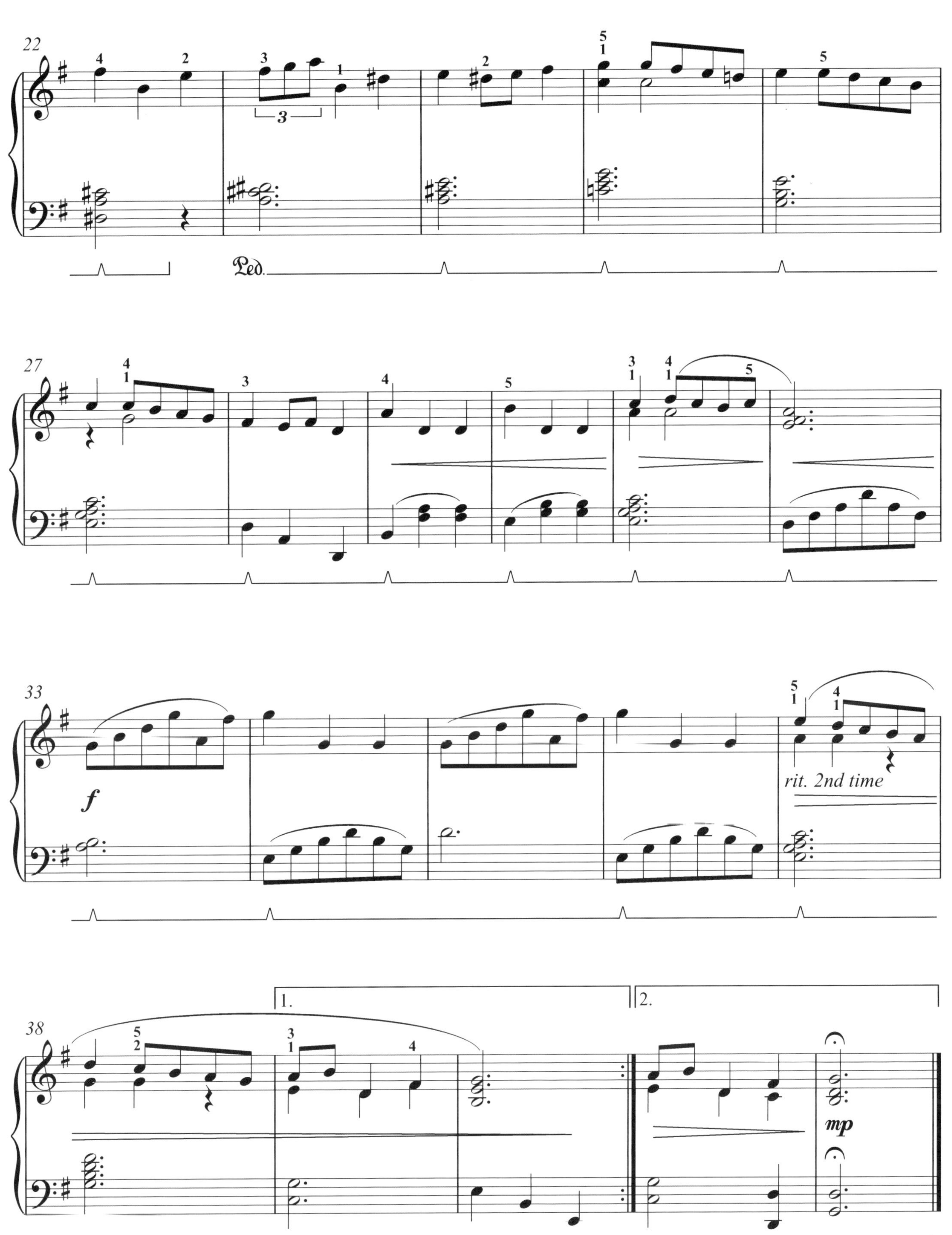

Ped.
f
rit. 2nd time
1.
2.
mp

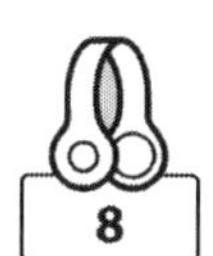

Musette

from the Notebook for Anna Magdalena Bach 1725
BWV Anh. 126

Johann Sebastian Bach
Arranged by Bryce Russell

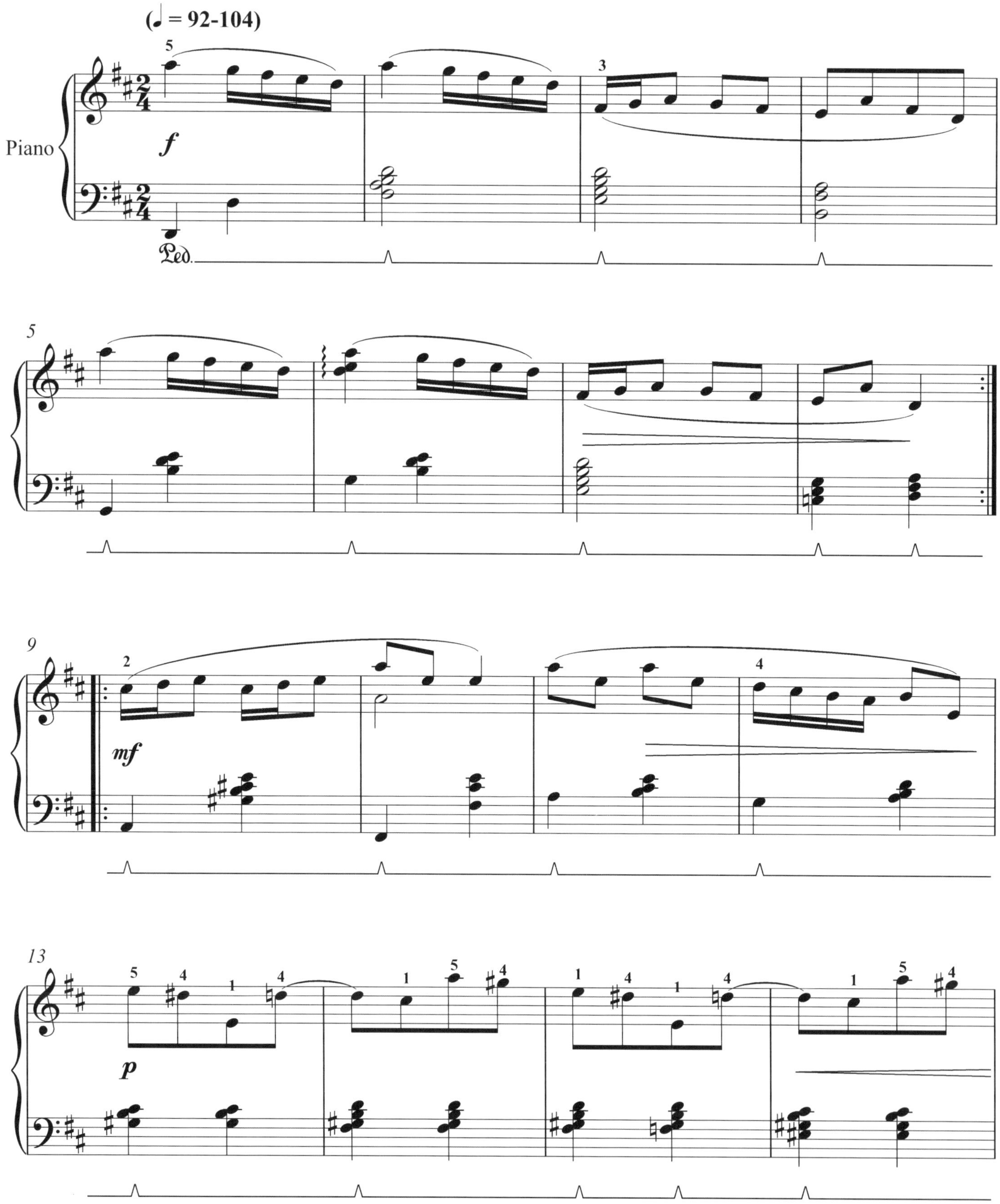

(♩ = 92-104)

Piano

f

Ped.

5

9

mf

13

p

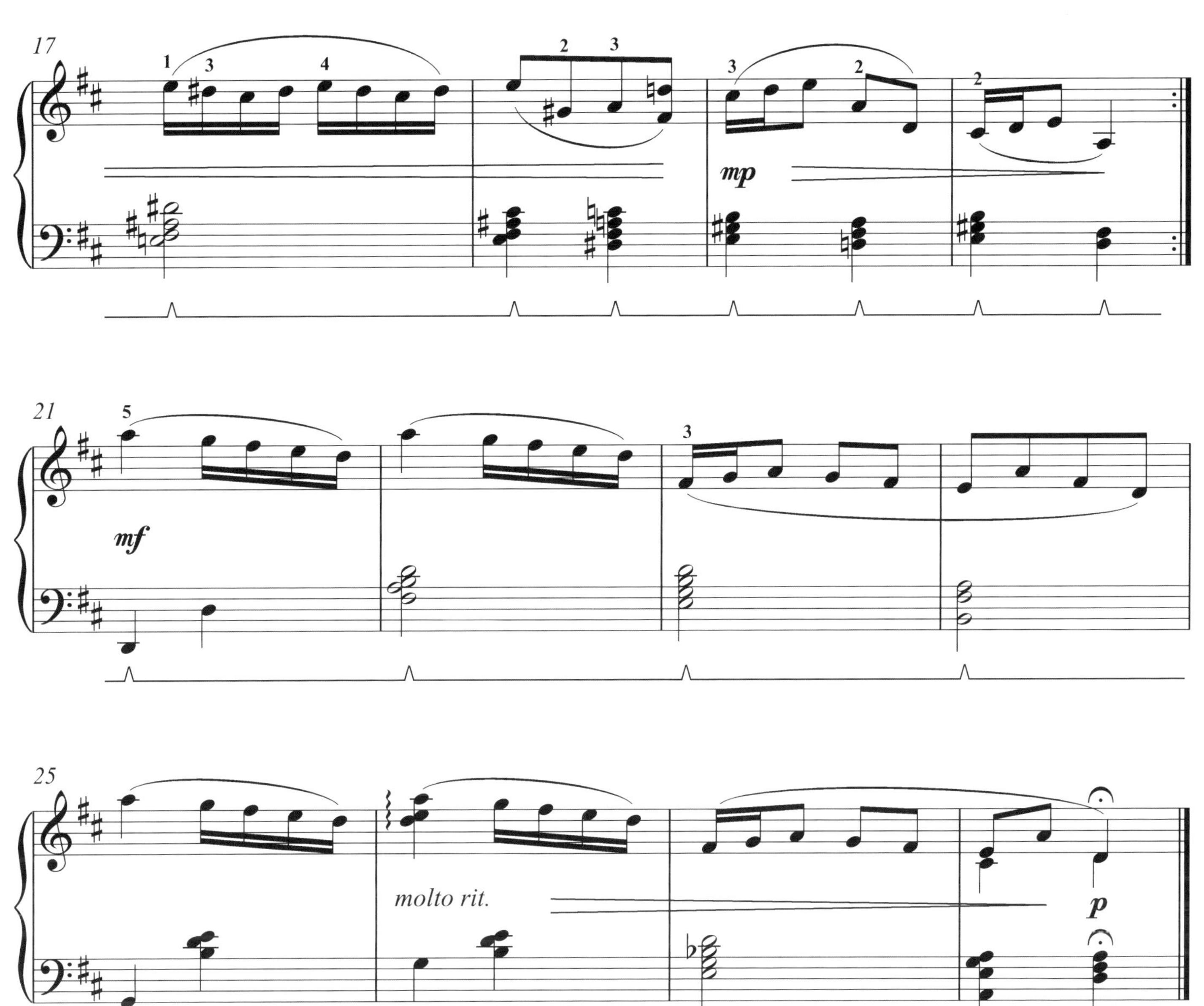
17
mp
21
mf
25
molto rit.
p

Polonaise

from the Notebook for Anna Magdalena Bach 1725
BWV Anh. 128

Johann Sebastian Bach
Arranged by Bryce Russell

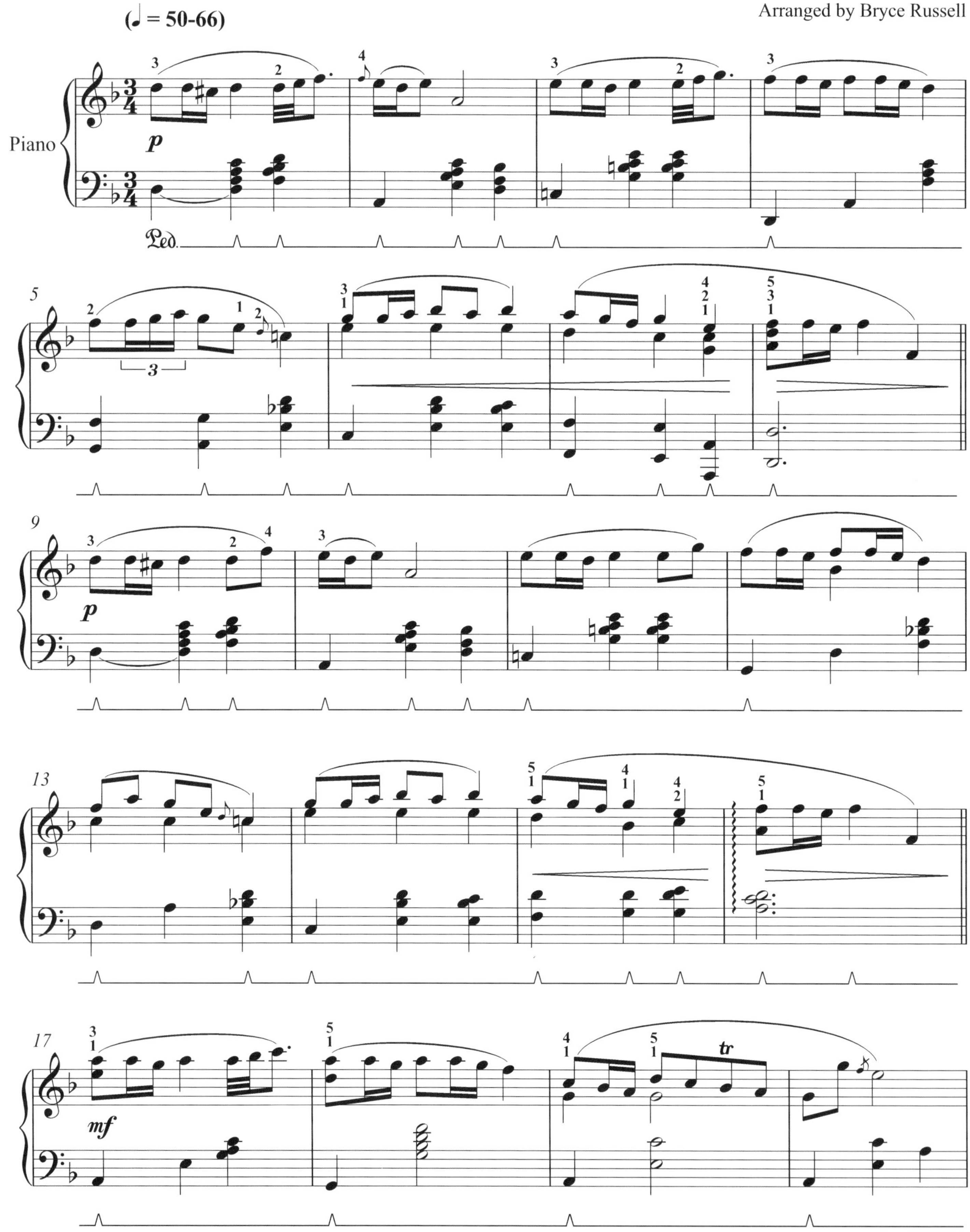

(♩ = 50-66)

Piano

p

Ped.

5

9

p

13

17

mf

tr

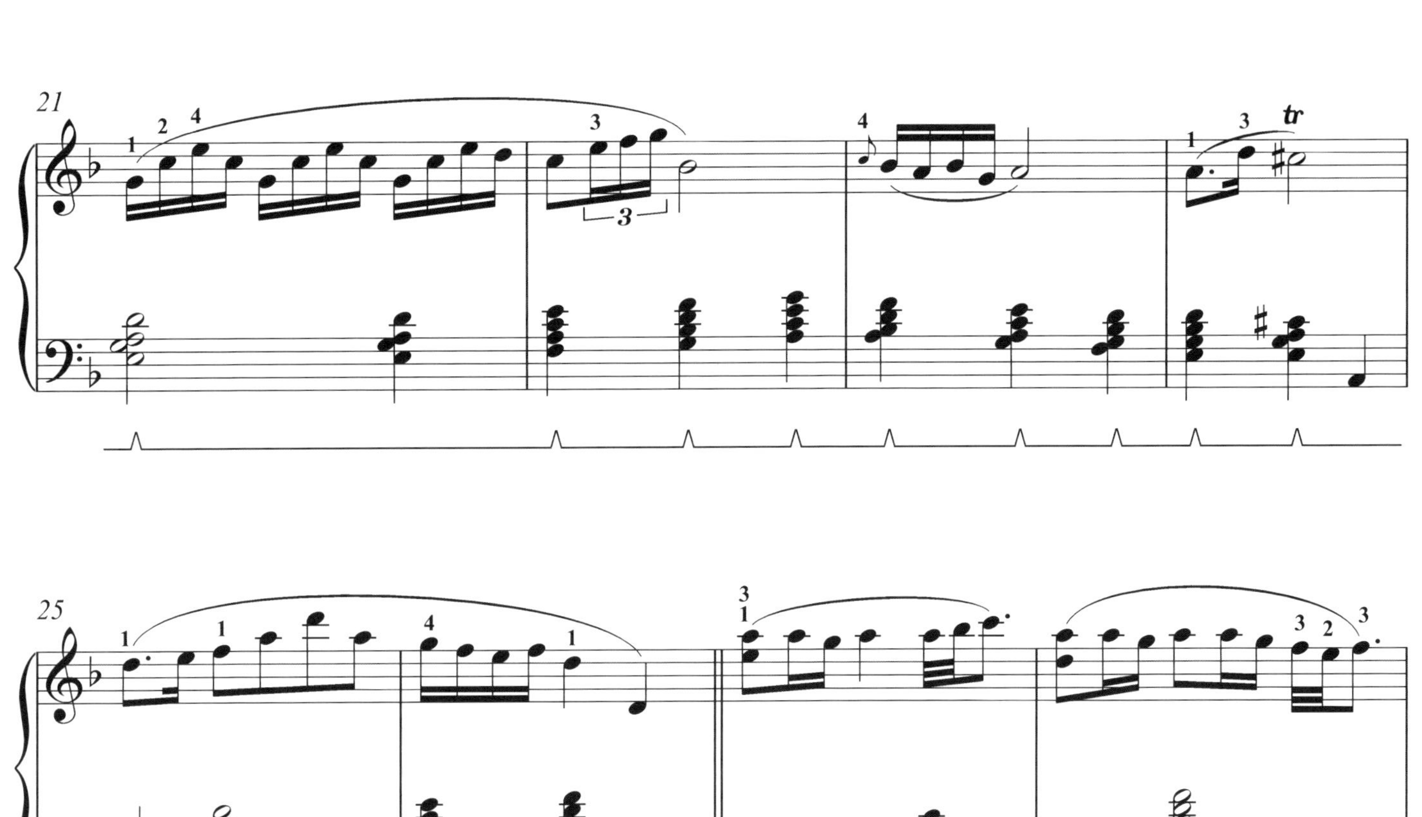
21
tr

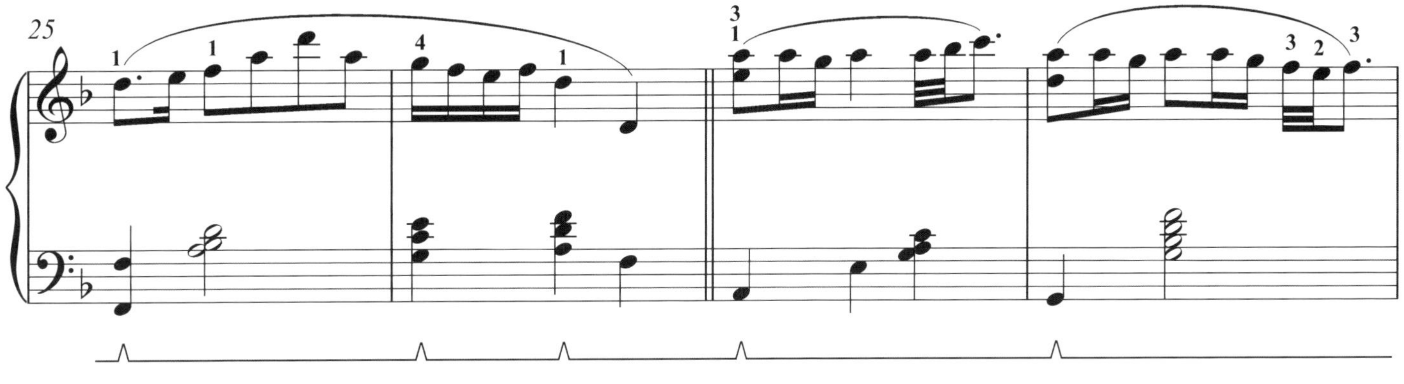
25

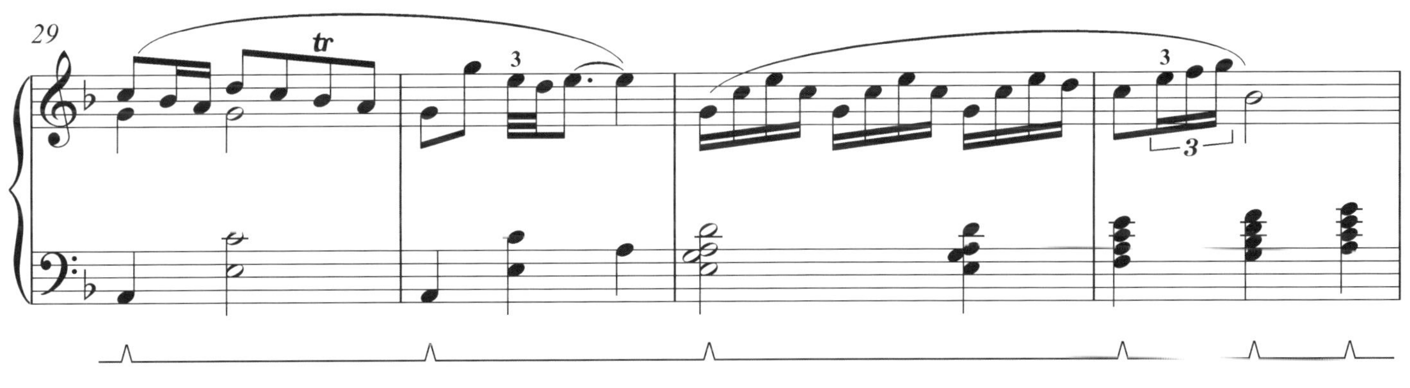
29
tr

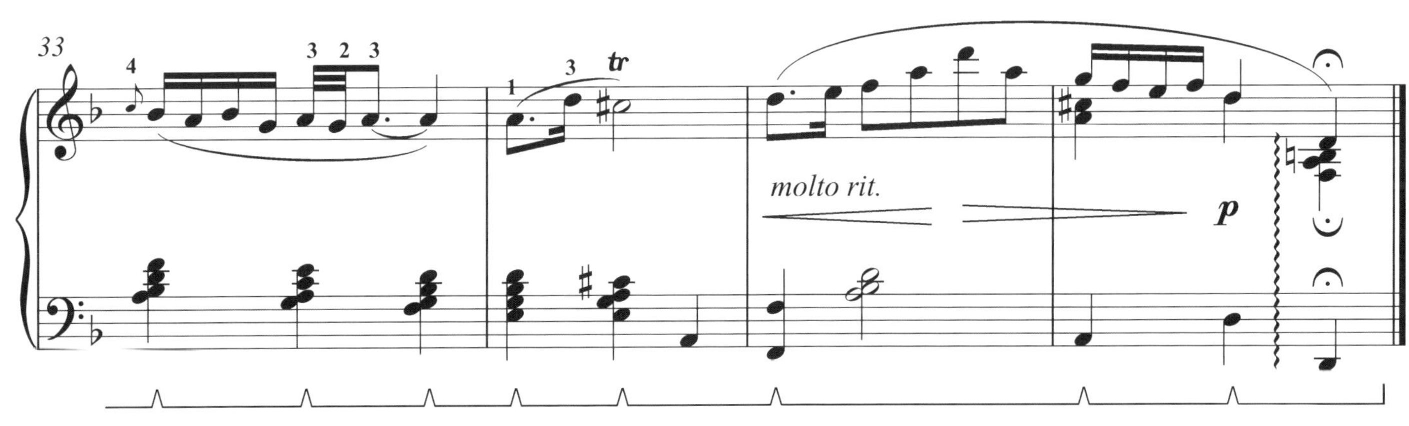
33
tr
molto rit.
p

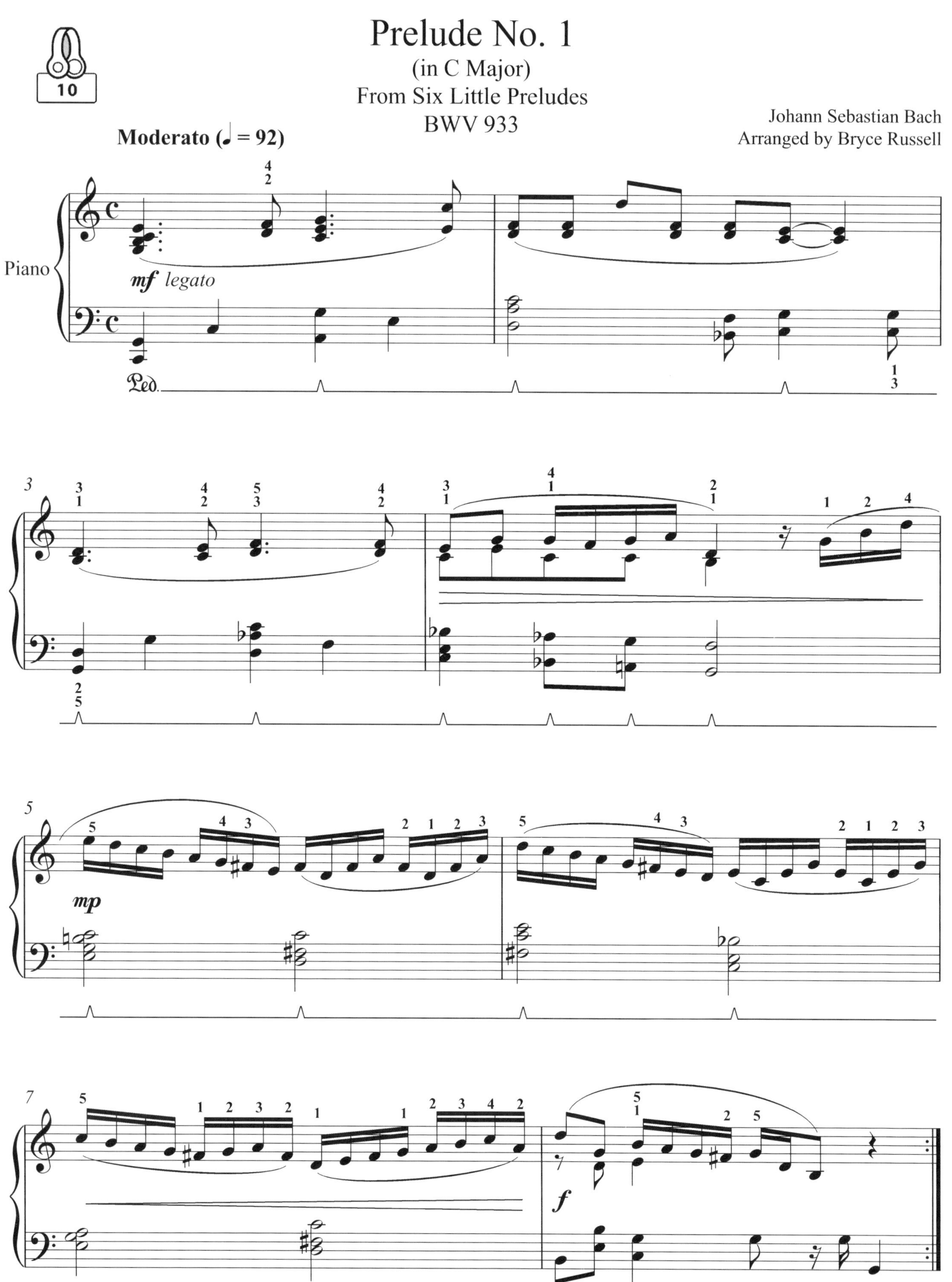
10
Prelude No. 1
(in C Major)
From Six Little Preludes
BWV 933
Johann Sebastian Bach
Arranged by Bryce Russell
Moderato (♩ = 92)
Piano
mf legato
mp
f

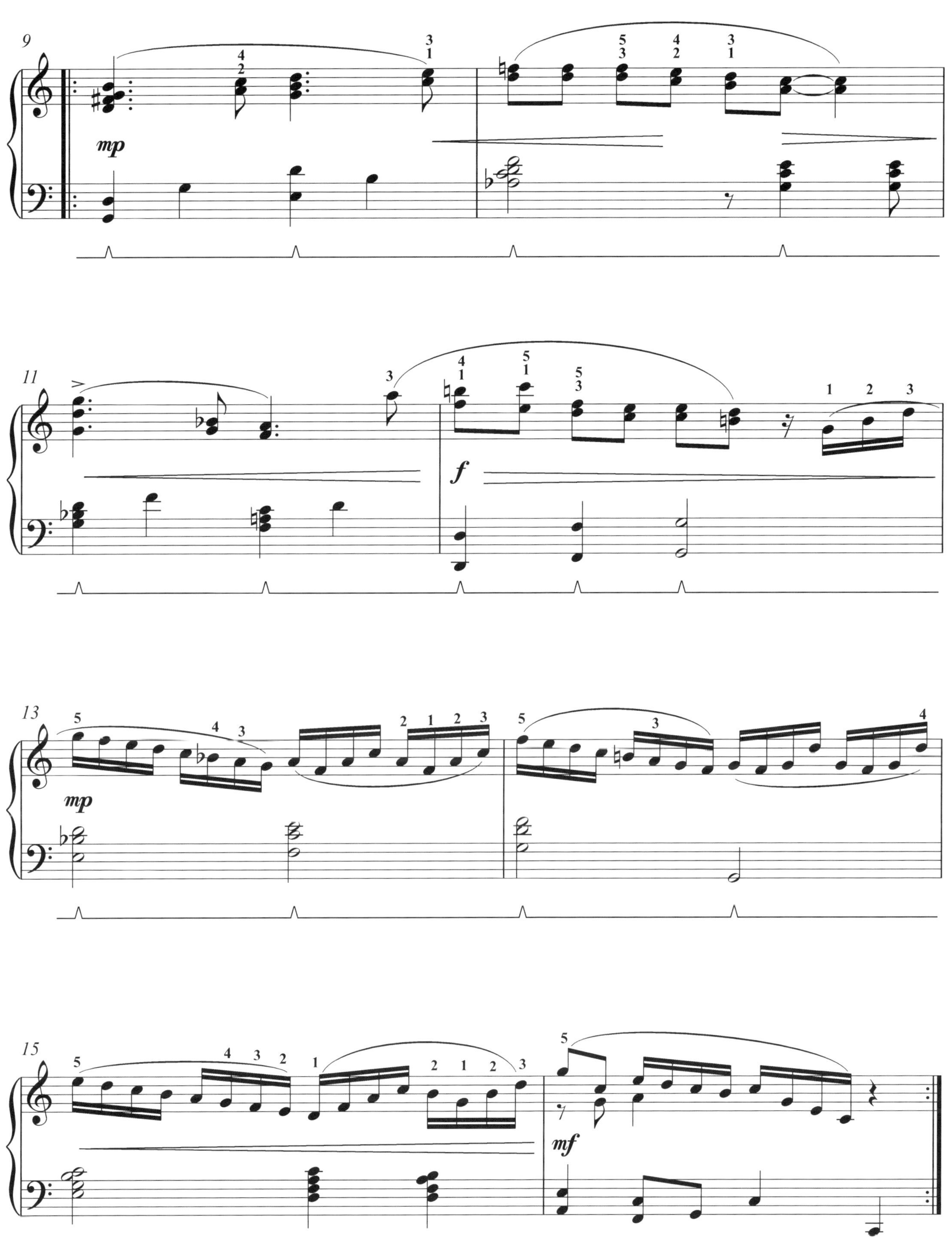
9
mp
11
f
13
mp
15
mf

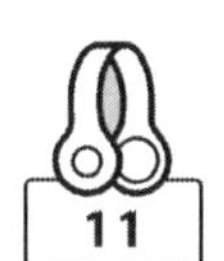

Prelude No. 17

(in A♭ Major)

from The Well-Tempered Clavier - Book 1

BWV 862

Johann Sebastian Bach

Arranged by Bryce Russell

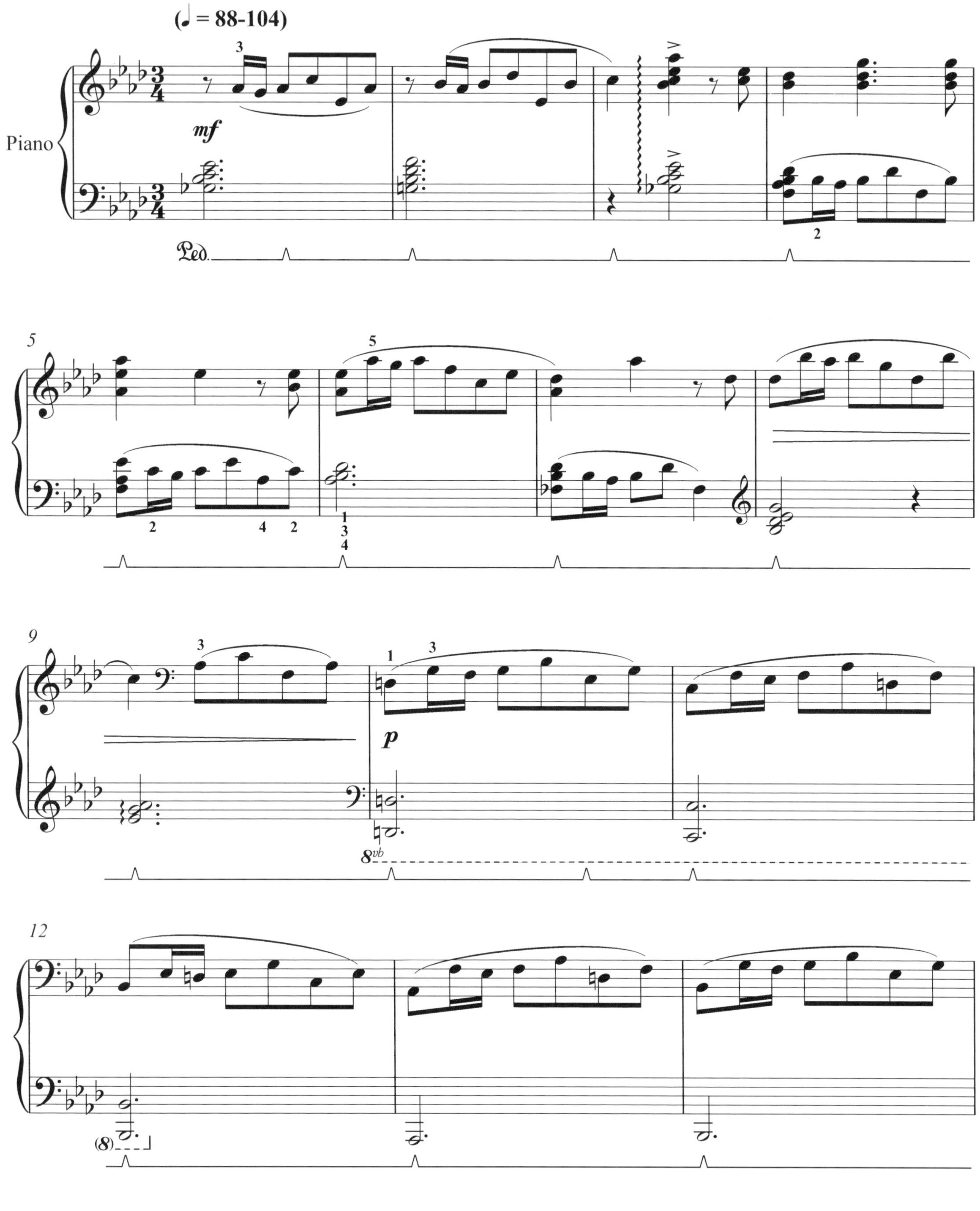

(♩. = 88-104)

Piano

mf

Ped.

5

9

p

8vb

12

(8)

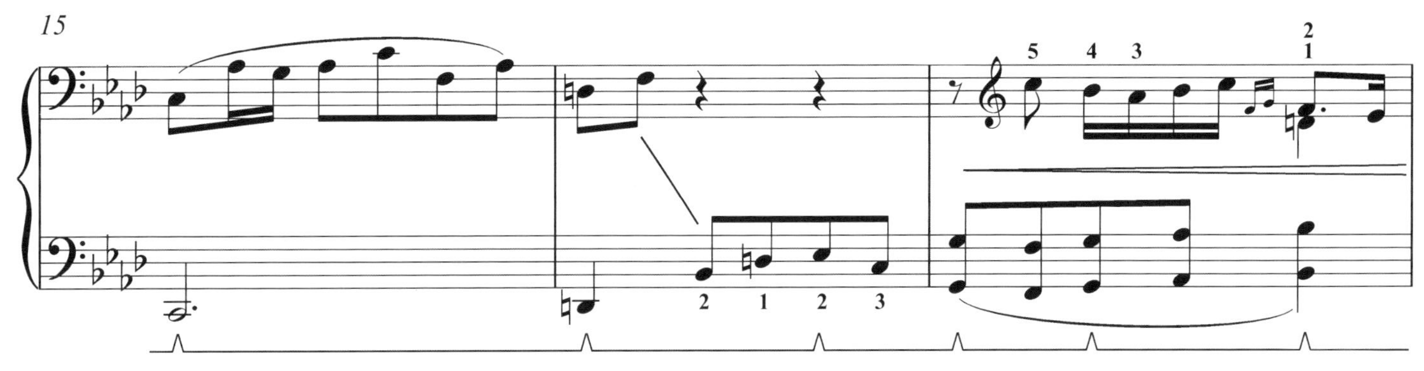
15
5
4
3
2
1
2
1
2
3
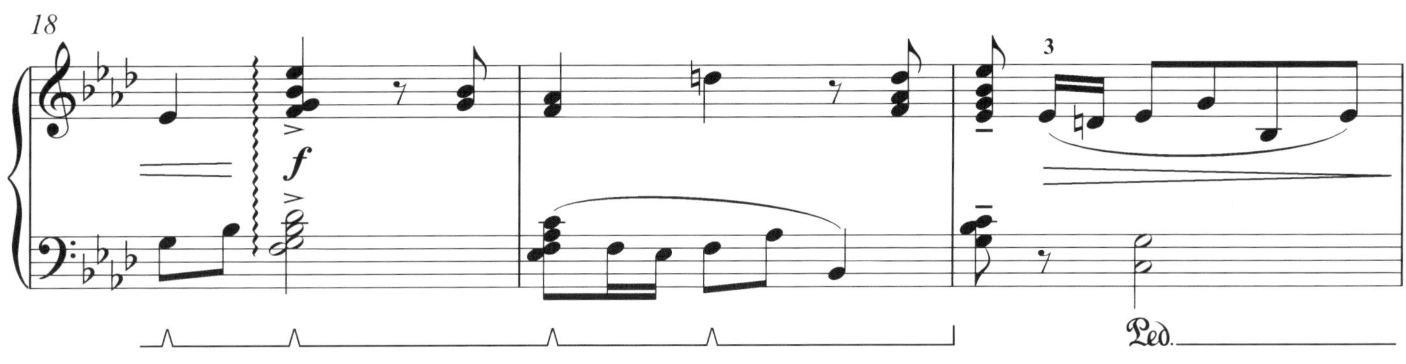
18
f
3
Ped.
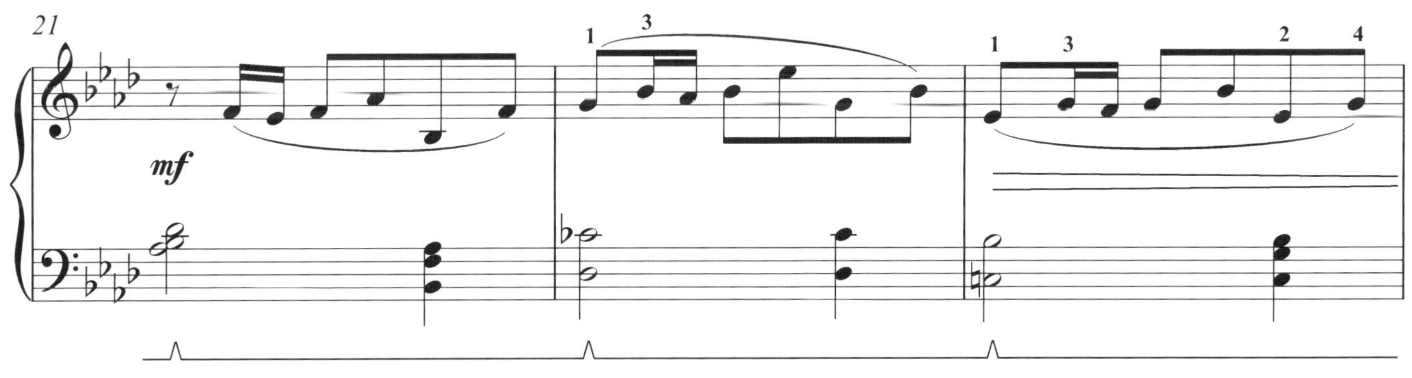
21
mf
1
3
1
3
2
4
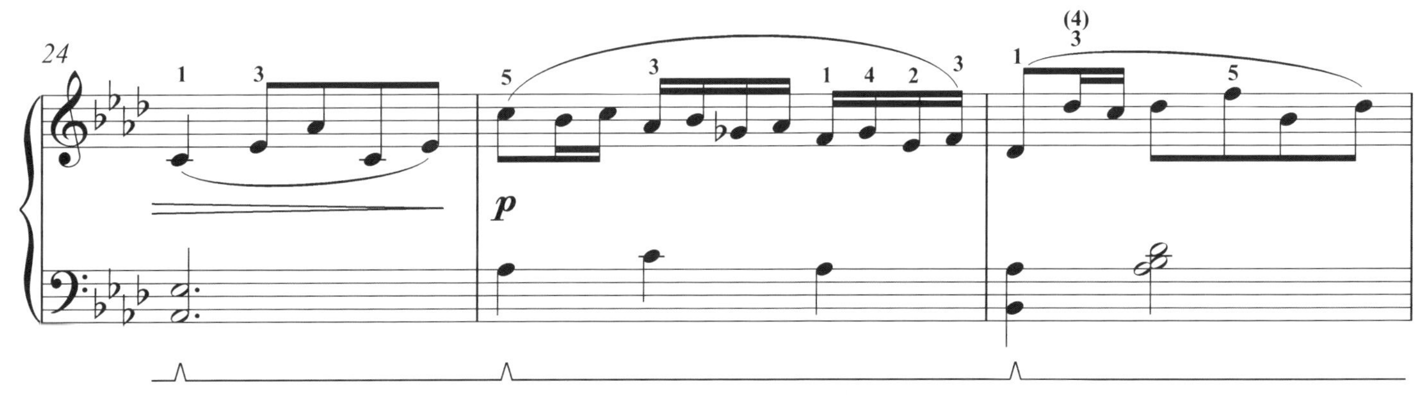
24
1
3
5
3
1
4
2
3
p
(4)
3
1
5

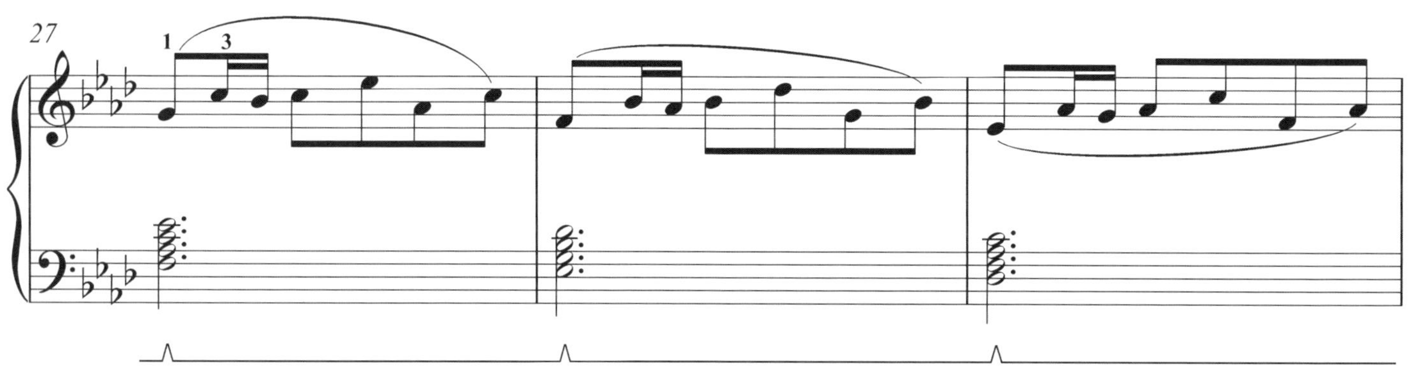
27
1
3
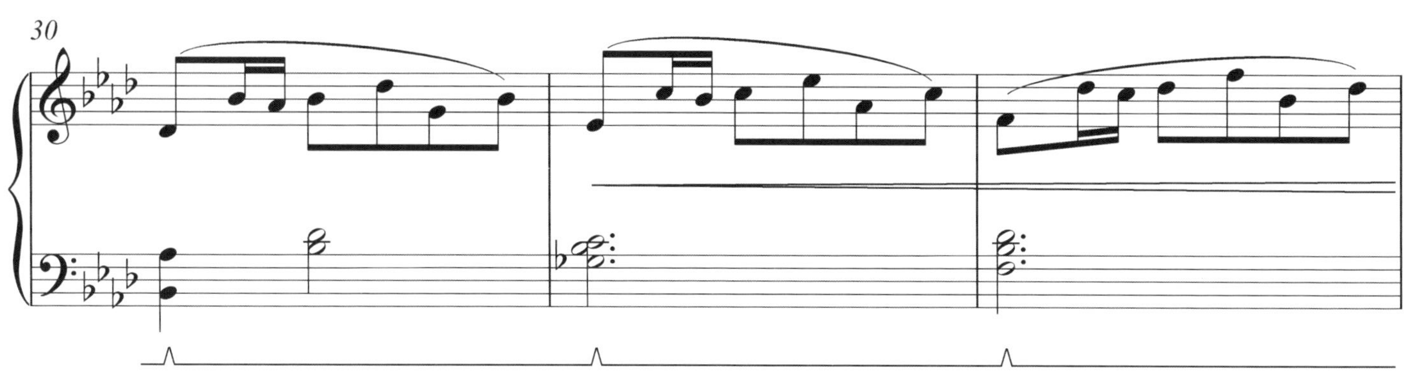
30
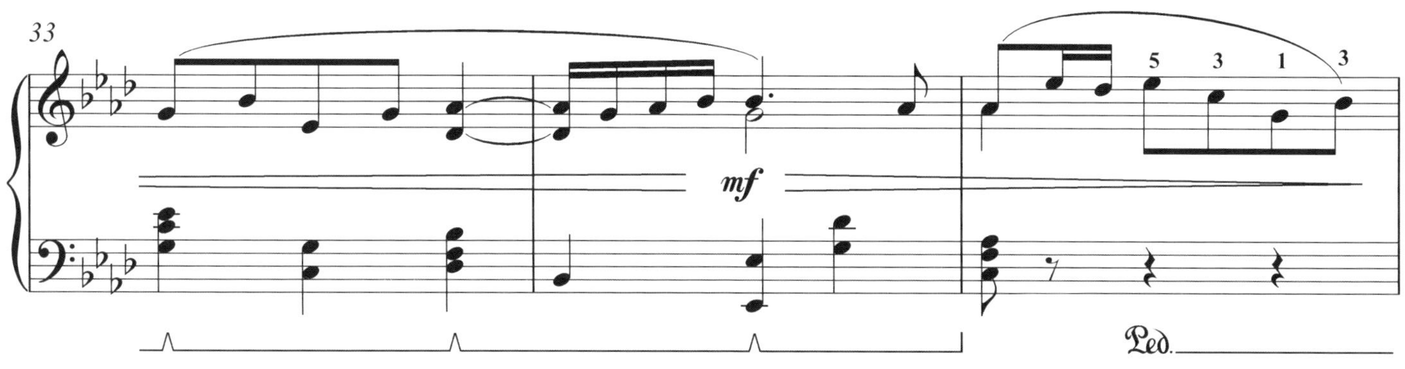
33
mf
5
3
1
3
Ped.
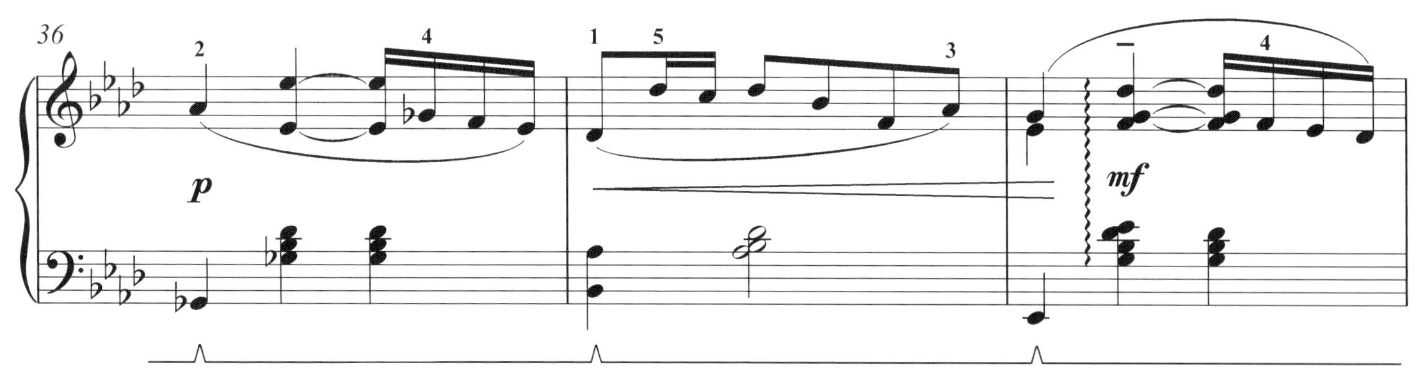
36
2
4
p
1
5
3
4
mf

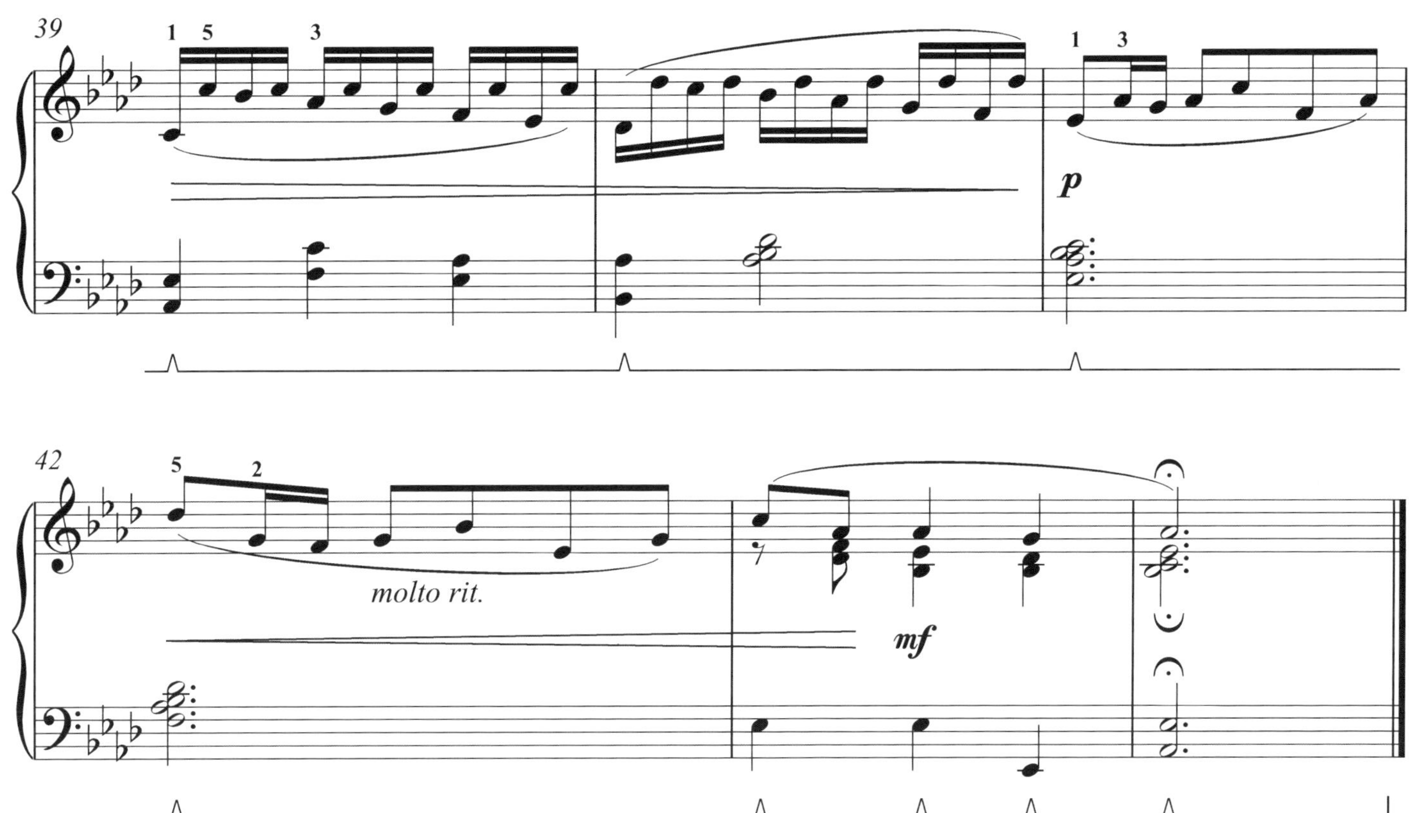
39
p
42
molto rit.
mf

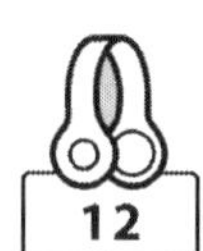

Sarabande

from English Suite No. 2

BWV 807

Johann Sebastian Bach

Arranged by Bryce Russell

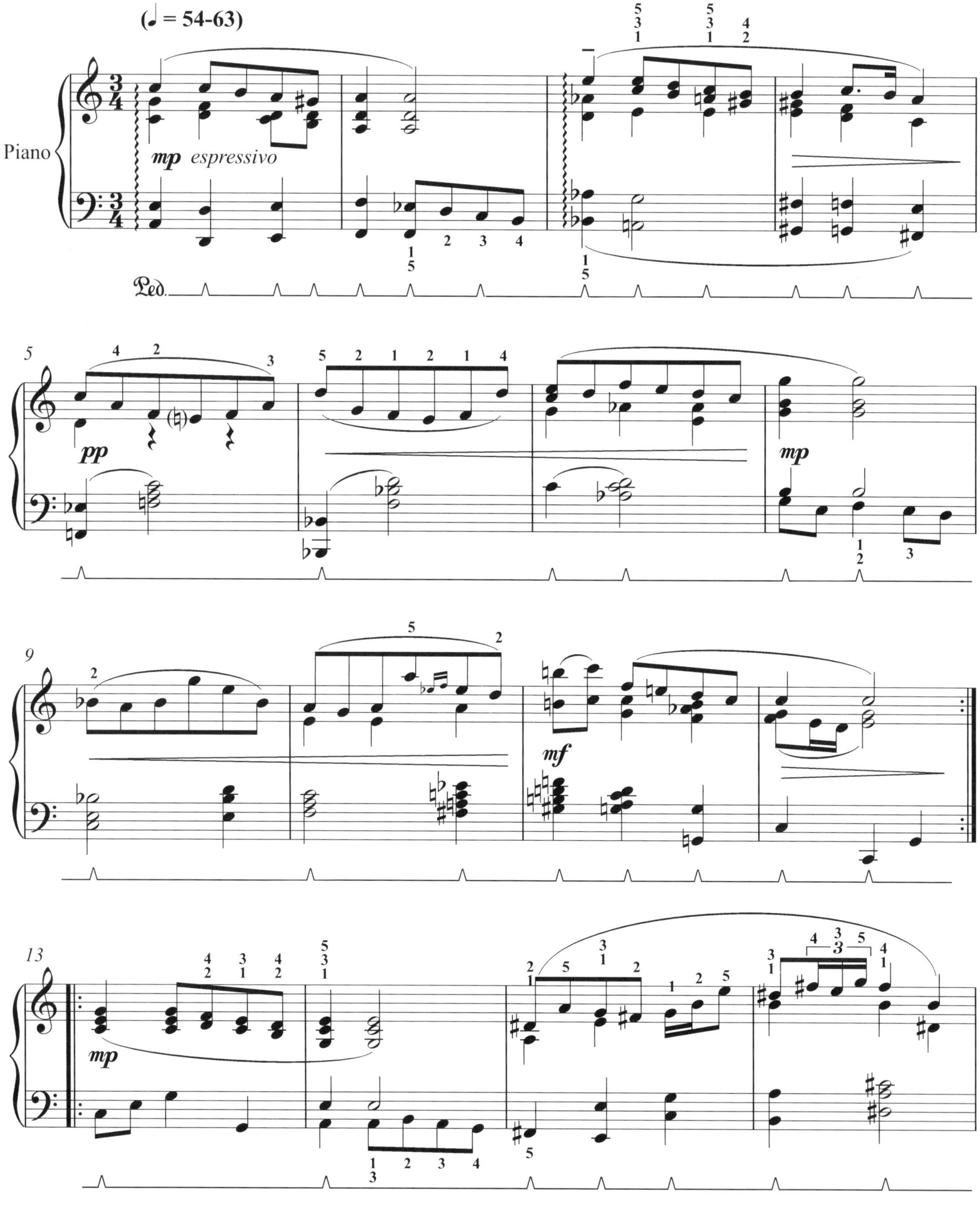

(♩ = 54-63)

Piano

mp espressivo

Ped.

5

pp

mp

9

mf

13

mp

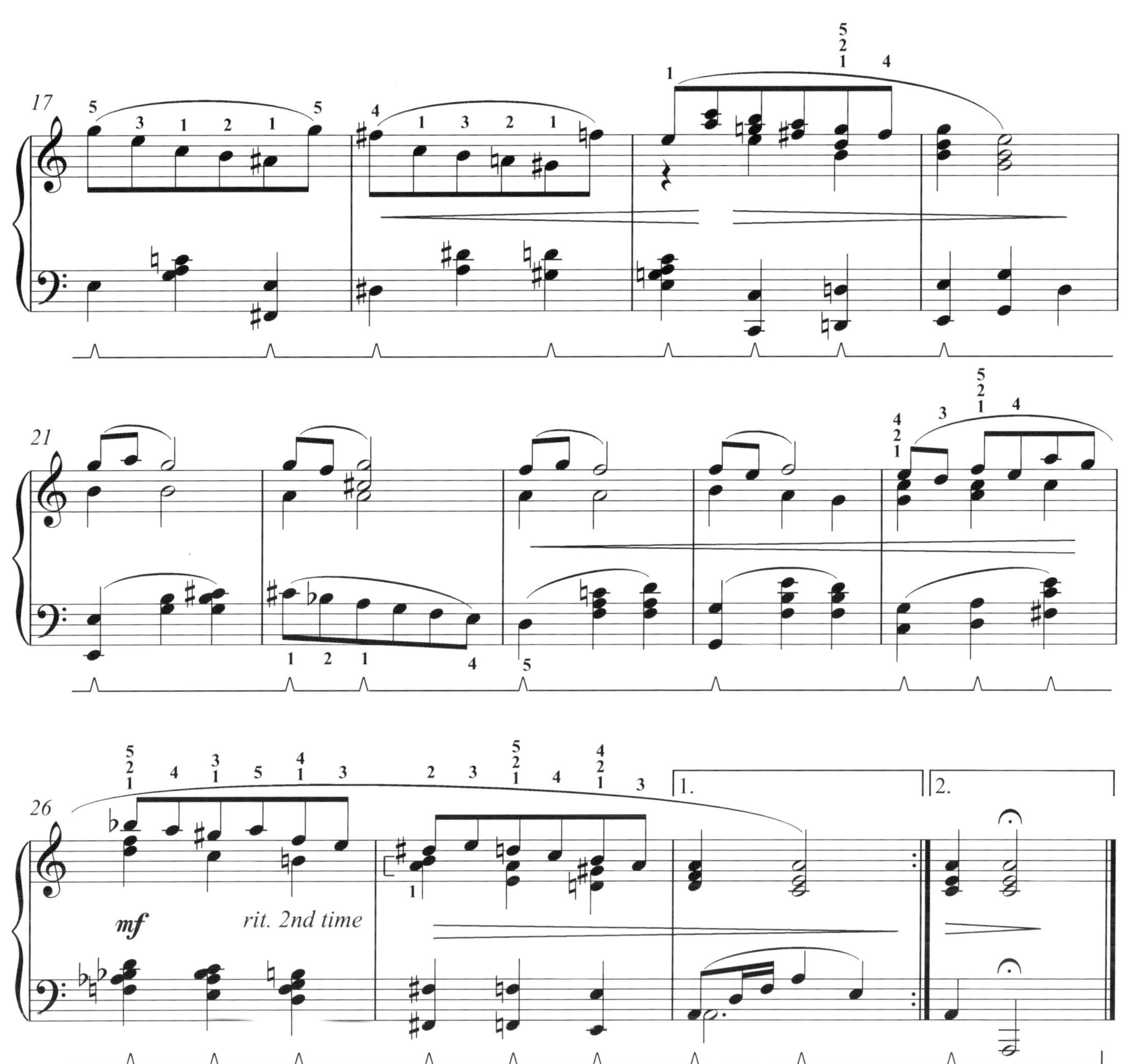
17
21
26
mf
rit. 2nd time
1.
2.

About the Author

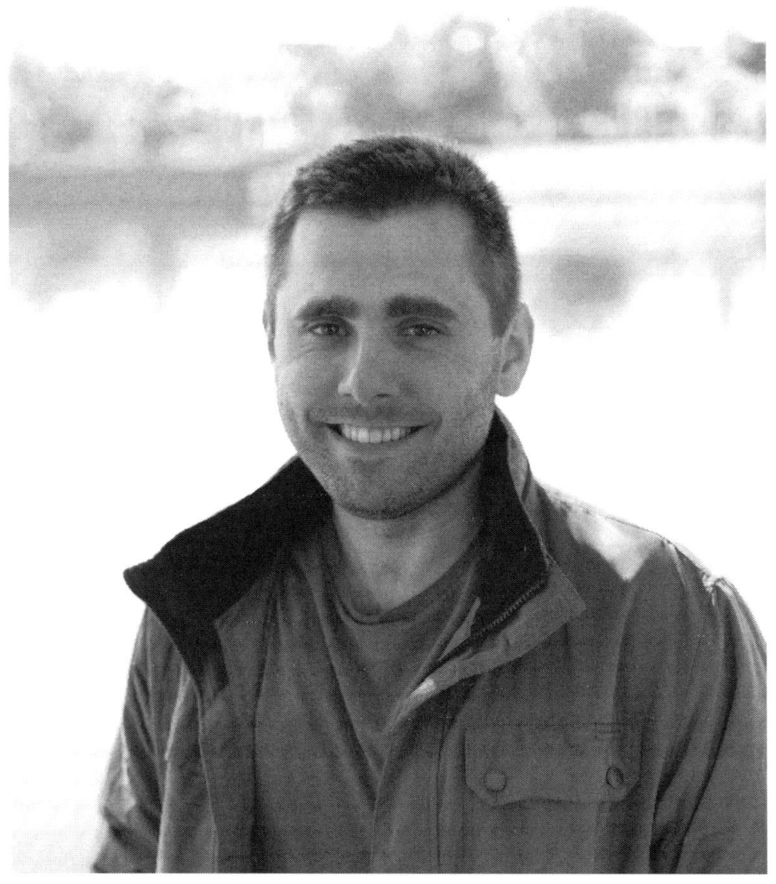

Bryce Russell is a composer, pianist, arranger, orchestrator, and author. Studied piano under Tahnia Lund and earned a Bachelor of Arts in music composition for film, television, and video games from Berklee College of Music in Boston, Massachusetts. While there, he studied with Ben Newhouse (Disney DVD logo), Vicente Avella (Family Guy & American Dad), Rick McLaughlin, Kari Juusela, and Eric Gould. He also earned a Master's degree in Curriculum and Instruction for Music from Southeastern Oklahoma State University.

Russell was a member of the Music Teachers Association of California (MTAC) from 2012 to 2017. He performed original music at MTAC concerts from venues in San Diego to Oakland, CA. Another composition, "Flying with Eagles" was recognized by the city of Los Angeles with a certificate back in 2012 and an invitation to participate in the Hollywood Christmas Parade.

His music albums can be found online at Spotify and Apple Music, including his orchestral/soundtrack album "MovieScapes" (2022). Russell is currently working as a performing pianist, composer, and author.

Other Mel Bay Piano Solo Books

Classics

Beethoven Sonatas Book 1 (Gail Smith)
Canons and Rounds for Piano Solo (Gail Smith)
César Frank Selected Piano Compositions (Gail Smith)
Clara Schumann's Piano Notebook (Gail Smith)
Four Centuries of Women Composers (Gail Smith)
Happy Birthday Suite (Gail Smith)
Great Literature for Piano Book 1: Easy (Gail Smith)
Great Literature for Piano Book 2: Elementary (Gail Smith)
Great Literature for Piano Book 3: Intermediate (Gail Smith)
Great Literature for Piano Book 4: Difficult (Gail Smith)
Ten Waltzes by Johann Strauss, Jr. for Solo Piano (Gail Smith)
The Life and Music of Edward MacDowell (Gail Smith)

Jazz and Contemporary

Anyone Can Improvise (Matt Dennis)
Blues Keyboard Method Level 1 (Barrett/Czarnecki)
Blues Keyboard Method Level 2 (Barrett/Czarnecki)
Creative Synthesizer Technique (Holzman)
Essential Jazz Lines in the Style of Bill Evans (C. Christiansen/P. Danielsson)
Improvisation Step by Step (Stefanuk)
Jazz Album for Piano (Stefanuk)
Jazz Exercises for the Piano (Paul Smith)
Jazz Piano Ad-Lib Phrases (Iwase)
Jazz Piano Chords (Stefanuk)
Jazz Piano Scales and Modes (Stefanuk)
Jazz Studies for Piano (Paul Smith)
Jazz Theory Handbook (Sptizer)
Jazzin' the Blues (Corozine)
Salsa & Pepper: Latin Jazz (Paul Smith)
Vijay Iyer: Selected Compositions (1999-2008)

Other Mel Bay Piano Solo Books

Folk/Ethnic/Traditional

Argentinean Tangos for Keyboard (Matthiesen)
Beautiful Airs, Ballads, Spirituals and Folk Favorites for Piano/Russell
Brazilian Music for Piano Vol. 1: The Choro (Medeiros/Lyra/Almada)
Brazilian Music for Piano Vol. 2: Sambas & Bossas (Medeiros/Lyra/Almada)
Brazilian Music for Piano Vol. 3: Valsa & Marchinha (Medeiros/Lyra/Almada)
Brazilian Music for Piano Vol. 4: Xote, Baiao & Frevo (Medeiros/Lyra/Almada)
EZ-Play Cajun Tunes for Piano (Simon)
French Tangos for Piano (Rovner)
Habaneras, Maxises & Tangos (Matthiesen)
Happy Birthday Suite (Gail Smith)
Latin American Songs for Piano (Newland-Ulloa)
Native American Songs for Piano Solo (Smith)
Patriotic Piano Solos (Gail Smith)
Roving Through Ireland (Voss/Traiger)
The Lover's Waltz: Piano Solo Edition (Jay Ungar/Molly Mason)

Sacred

12 Spirituals for Piano Solo (Gail Smith)
A Classic Christmas for Piano (Gail Smith)
A Country Piano Christmas (Archer)
Carols from Around the World (Archer)
Christian Classics for Piano Solo (Gail Smith)
Classical Piano for Worship Settings (Gail Smith)
Complete Church Pianist (Gail Smith)
Country Gospel Piano Solos (Gail Smith)
Country Piano Easter Celebration (Archer)
English Carols for Piano Solo (Gail Smith)
Old-Time Gospel Piano (Cummings/Whitmire)
Preludes and Offertories for Piano Solo (Gail Smith)
Southern Gospel Piano - Blessed Quietness/Songs of Comfort (Archer)
Southern Gospel Piano - Land of Rest/Songs of Eternity (Archer)
Southern Gospel Piano - Devotion (Archer)
Southern Gospel Piano - Giving Thanks (Archer)
Southern Gospel Piano - Songs of Faith (Archer)
Southern Gospel Piano - Lyrical Gospel (Archer)
Wedding Music for Piano (T. Price)

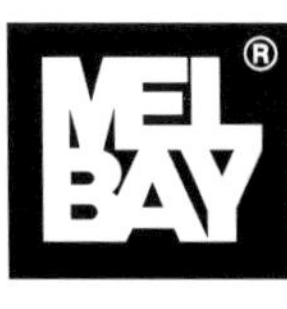

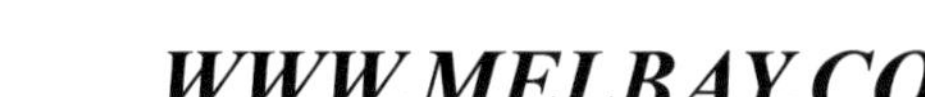